Seven Presidents and One Professor

Seven PRESIDENTS
and
One PROFESSOR

An Account of 72 Years at
Southeastern Baptist Theological Seminary

George Braswell
with Rachel Alley

Bennington, Vermont

Seven Presidents and One Professor

An Account of 72 Years at Southeastern Baptist Theological Seminary

Copyright © 2024 by George Braswell and Rachel Alley

Cover Design by Leason Stiles

Photo of Stealy Hall courtesy of Southeastern Baptist Theological Seminary

Published by Northeastern Baptist Press
        Post Office Box 4600
        Bennington, VT 05201

Softcover ISBN: 978-1-953331-37-3

TABLE OF
CONTENTS

FOREWORD

Mention the name George Braswell and any person who has been involved actively in Southern Baptist life over the last 50 years will immediately recognize him to be one of the foremost global scholars in Islam, World Religions & Middle East studies. He immersed himself in the Islamic world during his seven years of service as a missionary to Iran for the International Mission Board. He was one of only three Westerners to serve on the faculty of the University of Tehran in Iran, where he taught Comparative Religions in the early 1970s. It was there that he was able to see Islam through the eyes of its Mullahs and educational leaders, learning personally the culture of Iran. He was accepted by the Islamic leadership because of his careful and personal inquiry into Islam and its culture. After serving for 7 years in Iran, the turmoil in Iran itself led him to return to the United States. He became Distinguished Professor of Missions & World Religions at Southeastern Baptist Theological Seminary and served for 30 years. After leaving Southeastern he helped found the World Religion & Global Cultural Center at Campell Divinity School in North Carolina in 2007.

When I was president of the Baptist Sunday School Board, now LifeWay, we published seven of his books and, prior to my coming to LifeWay, three of his books had already been published through LifeWay. Here is a veteran missionary and educator who has distinguished himself brilliantly throughout his life. Now he has penned these pages you hold in your hand. He is one of a very few people who has had close relationships with all seven of the presidents of Southeastern Baptist Theological Seminary. He has presented to us a first-hand look at the founding and development of one of the finest seminaries in the world. His gentle, yet thorough, way is captivating and revealing of the birth and growth of Southeastern Baptist Theological Seminary. He carefully leads us in the maturity of the seminary through his relationship with the seven presidents.

While he has proven his abilities as a scholar, these pages are not difficult to read. This is the personal journey of one man with the presidents who have shaped and molded Southeastern Baptist Theological Seminary. George Braswell writes in a clear, often folksy, and always honest way. You will be blessed, enlightened and captivated by this journey of Southeastern Baptist Theological Seminary.

– Jimmy Draper
President Emeritus, LifeWay

PREFACE

This manuscript is a collection of memories of my personal experiences with each of the seven presidents of Southeastern Baptist Theological Seminary as well as brief historical background on each of them. As the only living professor who has known all seven men, I want to share my stories from Southeastern's history. All opinions are my own and only my own.

Some ask me why I wrote this manuscript. I wrote it out of my love for and deep appreciation of Southeastern Baptist Theological Seminary; namely, how each seminary president inspired me and supported me to be the best professor and teacher I could be in the classroom and outside it, the best researcher and writer I could be in publishing articles and books, and the best missionary I could be in teaching classes and witnessing to Jesus Christ with students and church members through out the states and in the Middle East, Africa, Asia, Europe, and South America.

The Great Commission has impacted my life as a youth, as pastor in Cullowhee, as Joan and our family were Southern Baptist's first appointed missionaries to Iran, and in my days as professor and into my present days. It is my hope that readers of this book will see the Great Commission thread throughout.

– Dr. George Braswell

1

Appreciation to President Akin

As a retired Distinguished Professor Emeritus of Missions and World Religions I am most grateful to President Akin for his every kindness to Joan and me, for his deep commitment to global missions, and for his providing time and space for an 86-year-old to recall cherished memories of Iran and seminary classrooms and colleagueship with faculty and with knowing and serving with the seven presidents of Southeastern Baptist Theological Seminary.

2

INSPIRATION FOR THIS WRITING

Shortly after the recent death of former Southeastern Seminary President Randall Lolley, I received a call from a longtime friend. He told me that I must be the longest standing "specimen" who served with all presidents of the seminary. I responded that I knew the first president and served with the remaining six. He then said that I should write about my experiences. Thus, the seed was sown, and the research and writing began.

Erving Goffman, a sociologist, published *The Presentation of Self in Everyday Life*. He used the imagery of theatre to describe the social interaction between individuals. In life one is on stage with prompts and costume playing a role, and the same person is offstage without prompts and costume perhaps living a role of a different kind. This view of human life may be referred to as dramaturgical analysis. Life is involved with a public appearance and the same life may appear in a private appearance.

Seven Presidents and One Professor

This writing will focus on my life as a professor on the public stage in interactions with the various presidents as well as interactions in more private settings. For example, how one might speak in a faculty meeting with the president might be different from how one would relate and speak to a president in one's home or on a tennis court with perspiration dripping down one's nose. Words and ideas might be expressed more personally off stage than on stage which might affect the relationships differently.

3

SOUTHEASTERN BAPTIST THEOLOGICAL SEMINARY

The Southern Baptist Convention was founded in 1845 in Augusta, Georgia. Within fourteen short years, in 1859, Baptists saw the need for theological education for the preparation of its pastors, missionaries, and Christian workers and began The Southern Baptist Theological Seminary which found its home in Louisville, Kentucky.

Southeastern Seminary had its beginnings in one building on the campus of Wake Forest College in 1951. The office of president, faculty offices, classrooms, library, and chapel were located in the present-day Appleby Building. When Wake Forest College moved its entire operation to Winston-Salem in the summer of 1956, Southeastern Seminary assumed use of all buildings and grounds which the Southern Baptist Convention had purchased from the college.

Since its first offering of classes in the fall of 1951 and its first graduation ceremony in the spring of 1954 until the spring of 2023, there have been 170 faculty members who have signed the Abstract of Principles and many adjunct professors. The alumni from 1954–2023 number over 18,000, and from 1954–2023 there have been hundreds of graduates appointed as missionaries by the Southern Baptist Convention missions agency.

4

BACKGROUND OF ONE PROFRSSOR

BIRTH IN 1936 TO SIGNED ABSTRACT OF PRINCIPLES IN 1974

My grandfather Braswell was a prominent contract builder of houses, churches, and motels in Emporia, Virginia. He had a fourth-grade education. My father continued that work. He had an eighth-grade education. I was a carpenter's helper for eight summers while in high school and college during the late 1940s and into the 1950s.

My grandfather and I listened to the nightly news on the radio. There was no television. He made me aware of national and international events. He attended Sunday School and worship services regularly. My grandmother ordered the series of *Hardy Boys* from Sears Roebuck for me to read. She sewed shirts for me.

My grandparents had a large acreage of land just outside of the town limits. They built themselves a house. They gave each of their six children the land upon which to build a house. Each did. In the early 1950s my father, mother, and I worked at nights and weekends to build our house with the help of others.

I grew up among uncles, aunts, and cousins in what was called "Braswell Town." We all lived in view of each other and weekly gathered at my grandparents' for a meal together.

I learned the values of hard work, an honest day's labor, being a good neighbor, surviving extended family quarrels among cousins, and of attending Sunday School and church.

The norms of the culture and society surrounding my early life were influenced by the churches and Christianity of a small southern town surrounded by peanut, tobacco, and cotton farms. Businesses were closed during worship services on Sunday mornings.

Invocations were given by local clergy prior to the beginning of football games. As president of the student body my senior year of high school, I gave the invocation over the intercom each school day. Marriage was sacred and divorce was a stigma. Family was honored, and respect was given to the elderly.

My father taught me to rabbit and squirrel hunt and to skin them for cooking. He taught me to saw lumber, to put up sheet rock, and to place roofing properly. He provided me the example of taking no short cuts in building a house and to give the customer an honest and full day of labor. He was limited in his "church going" but provided me the values of hard work, honesty, and love of family and neighbors.

My mother was a superb cook and relished cooking fried chicken, mashed potatoes, cornbread, and raisin pie. She worked at a clothing store. She also established a small grocery store and sold basically to the neighborhood. She did much of the business on credit, and her customers over time were unable to pay causing her to close the store. She could aim a twenty-two rifle at the tiny stem of a pear on the tree in our yard and knock it to the ground. She helped me buy my first rifle which I own today.

I was encouraged to go to Sunday school and worship services and Sunday evening youth training programs. I was most fortunate in my church to be influenced by committed Christians. My teachers and leaders were my pastor and his wife, my high school principal and baseball coach and teachers, my medical doctor, my dentist, the clothing store owner for whom I worked on Saturdays, and so many others.

Before we built our house in "Braswell Town" we lived in town "across the railroad tracks." Our neighborhood was mostly black families with a few white families with houses side by side. My playmates were black children and several white children. We together made our baseball diamond in the fields of a nearby cotton gin. Our bases were sacks filled with dirt. No parents were needed to supervise us.

The school for black students was in sight of our house. The school for white students was a mile walk. Segregation was the rule of the day. We could play together, and be creative in building a baseball field, and umpiring our own games without parental intrusion, but we did not visit each other in our homes.

Of all the cousins in "Braswell Town" I was the oldest and the first of the Braswell clan to attend college. My two brothers, Ronnie and Earl Wayne, were five and fifteen years younger than I. Both attended junior colleges. Ronnie was a Vietnam veteran.

My high school principal and superintendent approached me at the beginning of my senior year to consider an appointment to West Point. They knew the United States Senator of Virginia and assured me that the senator would appoint me. But I felt another calling.

My church leaders influenced me to go to Wake Forest College and licensed me to preach. I was able to obtain scholarships and work grants. In my sophomore year I met Margaret Joan Owen of Canton, North Carolina. We dated throughout our college years moving to Winston-Salem and married two weeks after graduation in 1958. I played third base on the freshman team the year the varsity team won the college world series in Omaha, Nebraska.

Joan's parents were medical doctors. Dr. Robert was a surgeon. Dr. Margaret delivered hundreds of babies in the mountains of North Carolina. The backgrounds of Joan and me could not have been in greater contrast.

Several seminal happenings for me occurred my last two years at Wake Forest. During my junior year my friend David Hirano, a senior of Japanese descent from Honolulu, Hawaii, and president of the student body, spent the Christmas holidays in my home in Emporia, Virginia. My family treated him as royalty, and he enjoyed my mother's cooking of baked turkey, homemade dressing and gravy, canned butter beans from our summer garden, and her famous raisin pie.

We then hitchhiked through the western mountains of Virginia riding with bootleggers at times to arrive in Nashville, Tennessee, to attend the annual Baptist Student Union convention. We met Joan there.

The summer before beginning my senior year while working in carpentry with my father, I hitchhiked to New York City to attend the Billy Graham crusade in Madison Square Garden and in Yankee Stadium. Joan traveled with a YMCA group of college students to meet with youth in religious gatherings across Europe.

I had been elected president of the Baptist Student Union to serve my senior year. The chaplain at Wake Forest sent me to attend a leadership conference in Green Lake, Wisconsin, where we three white attendees roomed with a black attendee and emerged as brothers in the service of each other. The major speakers were Dr. Culbert Rutenber, professor and minister, and Dr. Samuel Proctor, educator and minister. Dr. Rutenber was noted as a long serving professor at Eastern Baptist Theological Seminary and president of the American Baptist Convention. Dr. Proctor was noted as president of Virginia Union University, minister of Abyssinian Baptist Church in Harlem, mentor to Martin Luther King, and as advisor to the administrations of Presidents Eisenhower and Kennedy and Johnson.

Joan and I our senior year visited Southern Baptist Seminary to determine if after our marriage we would enroll. It was a time of controversy between the faculty and administration which resulted in the firing of thirteen professors which was about half of the faculty.

My professors at Wake Forest counseled that we not go to Southern Seminary, and they recommended Yale University Divinity School and sent letters of recommendation. New Haven seemed a world away. Perhaps my selection to Phi Beta Kappa and Omicron Delta Kappa and my service my senior year as president of the Baptist Student Union and Vice President of Student Government impacted my selection by the Yale committee.

We spent three years at Yale University Divinity School. I was enabled to attend Yale due to generous scholarships and work grants and the provision of work for Joan. I was the only Southern Baptist in my entering class of several hundred which included Roman Catholics, Episcopalians, Presbyterians, Methodists, and other denominations.

My work grants included one year each with the YMCA, with Yale University Psychiatric Institute, and with the First Congregational Church in Fairfield, Connecticut. At the Psychiatric Institute I was assigned as counselor to a young Jewish man. His name was Walt. His extended family included holocaust victims in World War II. Walt taught this Southern Baptist how to shoot pool. Sadly, he hanged himself one night in his room.

I studied under such giants in theological education as Roland Bainton, Kenneth Scott Latourette, Richard Niebuhr, Brevard Childs, Paul Minear, David Napier, and

Dean Liston Pope. My classmates included later United States Senators John Danforth and Gary Hart.

While at Yale, Joan and I heard Dr. Martin Luther King preach in chapel. We also heard the campaign speeches at different times of John F. Kennedy and Richard Nixon as they spoke from open convertibles in downtown New Haven. Our first child, Margaret Anne, was born at the end of our first year at Yale.

Following graduation from Yale, we began looking for a pastorate, and I became the first full time pastor in modern times of Cullowhee Baptist Church located beside the library of Western Carolina University. Segregation was still alive but Cherokee and black students were entering the university. During my five years they attended worship services, sang in the choir, and participated in other church programs.

In my interview with the "pulpit" committee before the church elected me as pastor, I was asked my view of race relations. I responded that I would preach sermons from the Bible, that I would visit the homes up and down the rivers and hollows, and that I would welcome to worship everyone from every background. Perhaps these were bold words from a twenty-six year old with a wife and young child to feed and the desire to fulfill a calling.

I remember giving special sermons at the church during critical times of the Cuban Missile Crisis between the Soviet Union and the United States; the assassination of President John F. Kennedy; Time Magazine's front cover stating "God Is Dead"; the Vietnam conflict; and the popular songs of Peter, Paul, and Mary.

An important time at Cullowhee was my introduction to Sam James, our SBC missionary to South Vietnam, who was on furlough and who led our church revival services. Sam was our friend during our days as Wake Forest College students. We sat up many late nights to discuss and pray about overseas missions, especially Saigon, Vietnam.

After five years we packed suitcases leaving behind deep friendships at the church and the university and became the first missionaries of the Southern Baptist Convention International Mission Board (IMB) to Iran.[1]

Joan and I, with our three kids, lived in dormitory facilities at Ridgecrest Baptist Assembly in the first sixteen-week orientation. There were one hundred missionaries with several hundred children living a boot camp lifestyle with classes from early morning to late evening. We were the only ones going to the Middle East.

To break the monotony my good friend going to Indonesia and I skipped classes one day which was a violation of the rules. We went to the nearby Black Mountain Golf Course and each paid our three-dollar green fee. To our utter surprise the Reverend Dr. Billy Graham came out, returned our green fees, played nine holes of golf with us, and prayed for our missions to Indonesia and Iran, and left for a crusade. We became the "heroes" rather than the villains of

---

1   The mission boards of the Southern Baptist Convention were previously named the Foreign Mission Board and the Home Mission Board. Today they are known as the International Mission Board and North American Mission Board respectively.

the entire missionary family and staff. The director quietly told us, "Can I go with you next time?"

We traveled to Iran with only suitcases and backpacks seeking a work and resident permit to stay in the country. Beirut, Lebanon, was our backup if permits were not granted. We set sail from New York on the Italian liner, the *Michelangelo*, docking in Genoa, Italy, and traveled by air from Rome to Beirut to Teheran.

I recently discovered that the *Michelangelo* had been built in Genoa, the land of Columbus. It had been in an ocean accident with the death of several passengers and injured multitudes prior to our sailing on it. I also learned that the Shah of Iran later bought the ship and turned it into an army barrack.

I wondered about the Italian explorer Columbus discovering new worlds, and about the dangers inherent in travel, and about the Shah's soldiers sleeping possibly in the same rooms as our family. We were recipients of the wonders and miracles of God. We are thankful for our safe journey to Iran.

With the assistance of missionaries with the Presbyterian Church U.S.A., we met officials at the Faculty of Islamic Theology of the University of Teheran. They granted us the official permits. I became the only American and Christian professor at the graduate school teaching Muslim clergy. I also held an appointment on the faculty of Damavand College which admitted only Iranian women.

I could never have imagined teaching Muslim preachers in the morning and liberated upper-class Iranian women in the afternoons.

After five years in Iran and receiving a surprising and unsolicited invitation, I accepted appointment to the faculty of Southeastern Baptist Theological Seminary in Wake Forest. Joan and I returned to the place we first met in our early years of college.

Now some fifteen years later after living with our first child in New Haven in a house with an Irish Roman Catholic couple who became surrogate grandparents, and on a street of Irish and Italian Catholics, and later living in Iran among a 98% Shia Muslim culture, we were moving to the Forests of Wake for a new beginning. We returned with our children, three of whom had attended The Community School evenly divided between Iranian and international students. And we were bringing back our fourth child, Becky, born in Teheran.

Now the rest of the story of the life of one professor with seven presidents will unfold.

5

President Sydnor L. Stealey
1951-1963

A Brief History

In 1951, Dr. Sydnor Lorenzo Stealey, the first president of Southeastern Baptist Theological Seminary, would help launch a Southern Baptist seminary in the southeastern United States with limited resources and a single building on a college campus. Despite challenges, Dr. Stealey set the foundation for Southeastern Seminary to equip students in ministry for decades to come.

Dr. Stealey's early years were spent in the Virginia and Washington, D.C. areas. He was born in Martinsburg, West Virginia, to Clarence Perry Stealey, a pastor, and Anna Jamieson Sydnor Stealey in March 1897. While he was still young the family moved to Oklahoma, and he spent his high school years dividing time between studies and working for his father's print shop where his father founded the *Oklahoma Baptist Messenger*.[1]

He began his college career in 1915 at Oklahoma Baptist University until 1918 when he spent a year serving in the United States Army during World War I. He eventually returned to college and graduated in 1920.[2] In October of that same year, he married Jessica Wheeler. They would have three children, two of whom would live to adulthood.[3]

In the time from 1920 until starting as president of Southeastern, Dr. Stealey taught and held leadership roles, at a high school in Oklahoma and at William Jewel College in Missouri. During those years, interactions with local churches impressed upon Dr. Stealey the great need for leadership in the church and he began to feel called toward ministry.[4] In 1922 he was ordained and soon entered Southern Seminary. He completed his ThM at Southern in 1927 and by 1932 earned his PhD at the same institution.[5] Then from 1932 until 1942 he served pastorates in Indiana, Virginia, and at First Baptist Church in Raleigh, North Carolina. Following his pastorate in Raleigh he was hired as Professor of Church History at Southern Seminary in Louisville, Kentucky. He would teach at Southern Seminary from 1942 until his selection as president of Southeastern in 1951.[6]

In February of 1951, Dr. Sydnor L. Stealey was elected by the trustees to become the first president of Southeastern Baptist Theological Seminary. Dr. Stealey and the first staff of Southeastern began their work June 1, 1951, and the seminary officially opened in September of that year. Not only did Dr. Stealey lead the seminary as president, he also taught the church history courses during its first year.[7]

During Dr. Stealey's presidency, the school would gain accreditation by the American Association of Theological Schools in June 1958 and grow its programs and course offerings.[8] Throughout the years, Dr. Stealey focused on developing education around what he called the "tripod" which included pastoral ministry, missions, and Christian education.

In building a school with such a focus, his desire to develop these three areas of emphasis were seen through the structure of the school at that time. Students were encouraged to remain involved in ministries while studying at the seminary. To help with this a four-day class week was established, allowing students to travel back to their churches Friday through Sunday in order to serve in their own communities.[9]

The seminary also focused its attention on training students to serve the local regions. There was a great need for rural church leaders and the school devoted several classes and programs toward training students to reach and serve those areas. Courses on the sociology of rural and Southern regions and field work emphasized this focus. The development of a Field Work department in 1953 highlighted the emphasis on the school's partnership with churches, the value they saw in practical experience, and the particular focus on rural churches.[10] Dr. Stealey possessed a strong heart for pastoral ministry, saying that it was during some of the darkest times of loss in his life that he realized the depth and need of good pastoring.[11] His passion for this ministry was evident in the emphasis placed on good training for pastors at Southeastern.

Missions was the second aspect of that tripod. In a January 1957 publication, Dr. Stealey commented, "We will emphasize missions on our campus just as much as we emphasize education and evangelism. These three must ever constitute the tripod of Southern Baptist strength."[12] The role of missions at Southeastern was key from the very start. Early on, Dr. Stealey brought in experienced missions professors and special chapel services called Missionary Days hosted visiting missionaries, professors, or mission leaders who would speak to the seminary on a missions-related topic. Often students would commit to missionary service during these chapels, and in 1955 the seminary saw its first graduate appointed to serve with the International Mission Board.[13]

In addition to developing strong programs in pastoral ministry, missions, and education, as the president of a new seminary, housing, growing a robust faculty, and increasing resources in the library shaped Dr. Stealey's efforts. Of the many needs of a young school, one of Dr. Stealey's greatest desires was to help financially support students through their studies. One *Outlook* publication stated that "One of the first concerns expressed by President Stealey when he took over the leadership of Southeastern in 1951 was that there would always be sufficient money on hand to see that no man or woman would have to leave the Seminary solely because of a temporary financial emergency."[14] A missionary fund established in the seminary's early years brought added attention to Dr. Stealey's desire to see students trained for ministry when he stated that the development of the fund "brings more joy to my heart than almost anything that has happened since we started in 1951."[15] He truly desired to see those called to serve be equipped for their ministries.

Dr. Stealey would retire in the summer of 1963 following health complications, and in his honor the administrative building on campus was renamed Stealey Hall.[16] Dr. Stealey's passion as the first president of Southeastern Baptist Theological Seminary could be seen in many areas of his work over the years of his presidency, but his heart may best be witnessed through his deep desire to support his students in their theological training in order to become strong pastors, missionaries, and educators.

BRASWELL AND STEALEY

Experience with President

I first knew of President Stealey when he was invited to preach in my home church, Main Street Baptist Church in Emporia, Virginia. My pastor had studied under President Stealey when he served on the faculty of Southern Seminary. It was during my latter high school years when I began thinking about going off to college.

President Stealey painted an inviting picture of Southeastern Seminary and Wake Forest College located together on the same campus in Wake Forest, North Carolina, and encouraged members of the church and youth to visit. As I recall he was an interesting preacher with a lot of historical illustrations.

When I enrolled in Wake Forest College in 1954, I roomed with a seminary student, and we lived in Dr. J. Allan Easley's house on North College Street. Dr. Easley was Professor of Religion at the college and former pastor of Wake Forest Baptist Church. Dr. Easley's father-in-law was a world-renowned Professor of New Testament and Greek at Southern Baptist Seminary.

My roommate told me stories about President Stealey. My roommate had one change of clothes and washed and dried them each night for the next day. He was "poor as dirt." He told me that President Stealey made it possible to attend seminary with a generous financial grant.

My roommate told me that President Stealey was known as a user of tobacco products, was assembling the very best professors to join the faculty and could be very formal on occasions. On the other hand, he was most accessible to students in his office.

I never spoke with President Stealey in later years. I am told that upon his retirement he and his wife lived in the house on North Main Street which Joan and I later purchased before they moved to Raleigh.

I have listened from a seminary archive audio to his last chapel address as he retired. His emphasis was upon how grateful he was for student scholarships and financial aid provided by individuals and churches so that no one would be turned away from admission because of lack of finances. I remembered the need of my seminary roommate and his appreciation for President Stealey.

6

PRESIDENT
OLIN T. BINKLEY
1963-1974

A BRIEF HISTORY

Dr. Olin Trivette Binkley served as president of South-eastern Seminary from the fall of 1963 until 1974. His presidency would push forward the growth begun by Dr. Stealey and further establish Southeastern's foundation.

Dr. Binkley was originally from Harmony, North Carolina. His parents were Joseph N. Binkley, a pastor, and Minnie Trivette Binkley. He was born August of 1908 and attended Wake Forest College, graduating in 1928. He was ordained by his home church that fall and then earned a degree from the Southern Baptist Theological Seminary in 1930. He went on to study at Yale University Divinity School. He would continue his studies and earn his PhD degree in 1933 from Yale University, during which time he was pastor of Calvary Baptist Church in New Haven, Connecticut, from 1931 to 1933. During his time at Yale, he met Pauline M. Eichman. They married on August 24, 1933, and later had two daughters.[1]

From 1933 until 1938 Dr. Binkley pastored Chapel Hill Baptist Church in Chapel Hill, North Carolina, and taught sociology for a year at the University of North Carolina at Chapel Hill.[2] In recognition of his influence on the community during that time, a church in Chapel Hill would later be renamed Binkley Memorial Baptist Church in his honor.[3]

Following his time in Chapel Hill, Dr. Binkley took a position as head of the Department of Religion at Wake Forest College from 1938 to 1944. He then served as Professor of Ethics and Sociology at Southern Baptist Theological Seminary from 1944 until 1952, the same school where the future president of Southeastern Seminary, Dr. Sydnor Stealey, was also teaching.[4]

When the new Southeastern Baptist Theological Seminary opened its doors, Dr. Binkley joined the faculty in 1952 as an ethics professor and also taught sociology. He was appointed Dean of Faculty in 1958, and he continued in this role until he was elected as the second president of Southeastern.[5]

Upon President Stealey's retirement, Dr. Binkley was elected to the presidency at the start of 1963 and inaugurated as the second president of Southeastern Seminary on October 17, 1963.[6] Dr. Binkley's background in sociology would influence a focus on addressing the social changes of the time, which would help shape academics throughout his presidency.

As president of a still young seminary, one of Dr. Binkley's lasting influences was on the school's academics. He served as part of the American Association of Theological Schools, including as its first Southern Baptist president from 1964 to 1966.[7] He greatly valued rich education and regularly emphasized this theme in columns he wrote for the seminary's *Outlook* magazine. It was during his years of service that the Doctor of Ministry program began in 1972.[8] He recognized education as one of the most valuable tools for adjusting to the changing world and spoke often of keeping in tune with the mind of Christ.[9]

Dr. Binkley viewed education as a method by which the changes of society could be better understood, the Christian could be better equipped, and the gospel could be more clearly communicated. In addition to the need to provide this Christian education to seminary students, the seminary also sought to train its students to become Christian educators, carrying on the tripod of missions, pastoring, and education emphasized by Dr. Stealey. In the 1960s the school added faculty in the department of Religious Education and announced a new track for the Master of Religious Education which allowed students to earn their degree in education at a faster pace.[10]

Other changes took place including a shift toward work in urban contexts. While the seminary's earliest focus had been on the rural churches, growth of surrounding towns altered training to include urban contexts as well. Southeastern participated in an urban study in Washington, D.C., beginning as a summer course in 1967 and eventually held a similar program in Raleigh, North Carolina, starting in 1969. The program sought to help students constructively engage in urban ministry and also learn about the challenges, needs, and positive approaches to such ministry.[11]

Dr. Binkley was a strong proponent of the seminary's role in churches and partnership with other organizations. He stated in a 1970 *Outlook* that "seminaries and churches are partners in the education of ministers" and "the vital relation between churches and seminaries is a major source of strength in the Southern Baptist Convention."[12] Partnerships such as those in the Urban Studies program which connected the North American Mission Board (NAMB), the state Baptist conventions, and Southeastern Seminary, exemplified such relationships.[13] Partnerships like these existed with the International and North American Mission Boards as missions remained central during Dr. Binkley's presidency. Students continued outreach, and numerous students trained at Southeastern for missions and served in missions after graduation. It was common for missionaries on furlough to reside on Southeastern's campus in several homes available for missionaries.[14]

In addition to the academics of the school, Dr. Binkley encouraged graciousness and servant-heartedness. He demonstrated this in his own life and invested in the welfare of others. He served as a trustee for the Baptist Children's Home and in later years donated a large number of books to their facilities.[15] Dr. Binkley also helped the Wake Forest Library, which needed new facilities, find a permanent location. For these and other services, Dr. Binkley was given numerous awards throughout his lifetime.[16] As president of Southeastern he emphasized strong academics and caring for our fellow man. As president he stated that "This equipment for Christian ministry at its best is attainable in a theological seminary which is in fact a community of learning, deeply rooted in Christian faith, thorough in scholarship, and vitally related to the churches and to the culture in which the churches are located."[17] Academics remained central to the church context in order to equip students to engage and serve in their ministries well, and Dr. Binkley set the example with his own ministry.

In his honor, the trustees renamed the campus chapel after Dr. Binkley in 1969 to its current name of Binkley Chapel.[18] When Dr. Binkley retired in 1974, he left behind a large legacy among his community and at Southeastern Seminary where he had served for twenty-two years.

BRASWELL AND BINKLEY

Experience with President

Generosity to a "poor" furloughing missionary family

I first heard the name Binkley from my father-in-law who was on the old Wake Forest College campus as a medical school student when Dr. Binkley was also a student. He said Dr. Binkley was an excellent student who went on to Yale University for further studies.

I first met President Binkley while my family was on "furlough," that is, home leave, for a time from missionary service in Iran. Joan and I had been appointed by the SBC

International Mission Board as the first Southern Baptist missionaries to Iran in 1967.

We returned in June 1971 on home leave for nine months to live in Chapel Hill and for me to study for the MA degree in Cultural Anthropology. We were to return to Iran for a second term of missionary service after classes.

Joan and I met when we were Wake Forest College students when it was in Wake Forest and Southeastern Seminary was located in one building. I wanted to visit the campus to see the changes when the seminary inherited the entire campus.

I met Dr. Luther Copeland who was Professor of Missions and World Religions. In our conversation he told me that Southeastern would introduce its first doctoral program, the Doctor of Ministry degree, that fall and encouraged me to take a leave of absence from the International Mission Board and enroll in the program. He emphasized that since I was teaching at the Faculty of Islamic Theology of the University of Teheran, it might serve my missionary career better to earn a doctoral degree.

I told him that I would have no income from the mission board. In short, he told me that I could be his "grader" (Teaching Assistant) which would provide a modest stipend. Then he took me to meet President Binkley who told me I could teach a class, Theology of Missions, which would also provide a modest stipend.

Then both President Binkley and Dr. Copeland told me that they would look out for preaching assignments to provide some additional funding. Lastly, they said that

Joan and I with our four kids could live in a missionary house on campus.

This was my first meeting with President Binkley. He was gentle in speech, gracious in manner, and generous to a "poor" missionary family who had every intention of returning to Iran for another four-year term of service.

In short, after much prayer and soul searching, Joan and I moved from Chapel Hill to the missionary house in Wake Forest in the summer of 1972. In one year, I completed writing a thesis and graduated with the MA degree in Cultural Anthropology from UNC Chapel Hill; I completed a Doctor of Ministry degree and graduated in the first DMin seminary class, both graduations held in May 1973.

Interestingly, Sam James was on furlough from his missionary service in Vietnam and graduated with me in this first seminary Doctor of Ministry class. Just as our paths crossed at Wake Forest College and in my pastorate at Cullowhee Baptist Church, so they would cross multiple times in the future.

Often, I have wondered how my family and I lived through this rigorous schedule.

I also wondered why Dr. Binkley encouraged us and had faith in us and provided for us a house, a teaching assignment, and preaching assignments. He and Dr. Copeland made it possible for us to be better prepared to return as missionaries to a 98% Muslim country. These two gentlemen had a special vision for missions and for deep support of our family.

Special memories come to mind the year we lived in the missionary house on campus. At Christmas time a knock came on our missionary house door. It was a cold December night. Joan and I opened the door. There stood President Binkley with a huge Christmas basket of fruits and a very special box of warm cakes and cookies baked by Mrs. Binkley. He wished for us with prayers a very good Christmas. Then at spring graduation as he handed me the Doctor of Ministry diploma, he wished my family safe travel and generosity of Spirit upon our departure to Iran.

A Surprise Call and Offer

Our family returned to Iran in August 1973, taking only suitcases and backpacks and vacating the missionary house in Wake Forest for another four-year term of missionary service with the SBC International Mission Board. I would teach at the Faculty of Islamic Theology of the University of Teheran and begin a new assignment as Professor of Western Civilization at Damavand College. Damavand College was founded and operated by the Presbyterian Mission. The Shah of Iran was a patron as well as other leading Iranian government officials. The college offered upper-class Iranian women a liberal arts education. I also served as Associate Director of Armaghan Institute operated by the Presbyterian Mission. Six hundred upper high school and university students enrolled to study English. The Bible was used as a textbook for learning English.

Our family settled in a rental house; Joan shopped for furniture; and Margaret Anne, Robbie, and Brien enrolled once again in their favorite school, The Community School, which was half Iranian and half international students. Becky who was born in Teheran in 1969 was at home.

Within a month of our return to Iran, news came of a serious job-related accident to my father who was hospitalized in Richmond, Virginia. I quickly flew to Richmond and was at his bedside when he died. Leaving my mother in Emporia, Virginia, I rushed back to Teheran to start my teaching assignments and to thank Joan and the kids for settling into the house and school schedule.

In January 1974 the five million population of Teheran experienced an unusual snow and ice storm; the city had two snowplows. Joan was out shopping, slipped on the icy pavement, was hospitalized, and had back surgery.

In the spring of 1974, I received a telephone call from Dr. Raymond Brown, Dean at Southeastern Seminary, informing me on behalf of President Binkley that they would like to submit my name to the Board of Trustees in its meeting in April to join the faculty. Dr. Brown said that President Binkley asked us to seriously consider this invitation and pray about it and said that President Binkley would call back in two weeks.

What a great surprise! I was not aware of a faculty vacancy and certainly had not applied for any position. Joan and I had really just settled in for a long term of service with the mission board. To be teaching Muslim male preachers and upper-class wealthy Iranian women and high school and university students in English from the Bible was exciting, meaningful, and bearing Christian witness. Our kids loved their return to the community school.

And now President Binkley had so much confidence in us to ask us to join the seminary faculty. Joan and I asked ourselves all kinds of questions. What was God's will for our lives? Why out of the blue would President Binkley initiate such an invitation to us just after leaving Wake Forest and studies at the seminary? What about our kids who since 1971 had been enrolled yearly in different schools?

After much prayer and after communicating with our mission board director, Dr. J. D. Hughey, who encouraged us to be open to the will of God for us, we made a decision. (Please see Dr. Hughey's foreword in my first published book, *To Ride A Magic Carpet*). When President Binkley called in two weeks, we told him we felt positive about joining the faculty. He expressed his joy in our positive response and said he would be sending us a letter with details after the trustee meeting.

We had great respect and admiration for President Binkley and trusted his judgements and God's calling to make this positive response into much of the unknown future. We would have to pack up and say farewells to all our friends and depart for the States if the trustees affirmed President Binkley's recommendation. In April we received a call from President Binkley of congratulations. We would become a part of the Southeastern family.

Dean Ray Brown in his first telephone call to me in Teheran indicated that if I were elected to the faculty that I would have to complete the PhD to be considered for tenure.

Another Surprise: Binkley no Longer President

We were greatly surprised when we arrived in Wake Forest to reside in a small seminary house adjacent to the steam plant in August 1974 to learn that President Binkley had retired in May. And so the gentle, kind, scholarly man who had chosen and encouraged me and had been most responsible for bringing me from Iran to the Southeastern faculty in 1974, was no longer president.

Years Later, Dr. Binkley's Wisdom Given to Me

Years afterwards I would converse with Dr. Binkley after Wake Forest Baptist Church services and in various social settings. He was always asking about my classes and students, research, writings, and my speaking in churches and taking students on mission trips. Dr. and Mrs. Binkley had moved from the president's home to a small house across the street.

Looking back I remember a vital conversation with President Binkley in his home in 1989. Dr. Binkley had long retired. He had been most responsible in bringing me from Iran to the Southeastern faculty in 1974.

I had received an invitation by the administration and faculty of Southern Baptist Theological Seminary in Louisville, Kentucky, to interview for the Carver Barnes endowed chair of missions. They were ready to fly Joan and me out for an interview visit. It was the transitional era in the life of Southeastern with the departure of President Lolley and the entrance of President Drummond.

Dr. Binkley had taught at Southern Seminary before coming to Southeastern. He looked at me with his gentle face and told me what an honor it would be to be considered for the endowed chair. Then he assured me that I would be most likely elected to it. He then said that he felt I was needed at Southeastern at that crucial time in its history and prayed that Joan and I would consider remaining on the Southeastern faculty. With this counsel fresh on our minds, we thanked Southern Seminary for the invitation to meet with their faculty and chose to remain at Southeastern.

Dr. and Mrs. Binkley moved from their house to an assisted living home in Wake Forest. Joan and I often visited them carrying flowers and home baked goodies. They were always gracious, asking about our four children and our life at the seminary and the church. In latter days we attended their funeral services. Joan had served with Mrs. Binkley in the Garden Club of Wake Forest and on the Board of the Wake Forest College Museum and Historical Society. They always had much to talk about.

It has always been a mystery to me why and how Dr. Binkley initiated the relationship with me to join the seminary faculty.

Dr. Binkley graduated from Wake Forest College, and Joan and I met on the old campus as students. Dr. Binkley graduated from Yale University. So did I. Dr. Binkley served as pastor of a church in Chapel Hill and taught at UNC Chapel Hill. We lived in Chapel Hill and attended the church he had pastored decades before, and I studied at UNC Chapel Hill.

President Binkley was a man of prayer and deep spirituality. He in God's providence reached out to me in multiple ways and at the right time called me to respond to another expression of ministry. Joan and I are forever grateful to this Christian gentleman and dedicated servant of Jesus Christ.

7

PRESIDENT
W. RANDALL LOLLEY
1974-1988

A BRIEF HISTORY

The summer of 1974 brought the beginning of Dr. Randall Lolley's presidency at Southeastern Baptist Theological Seminary. He would be the school's third president and serve for fourteen years.

William Randall Lolley was born in Troy, Alabama, in June 1931. He married Clara Lou Jacobs in 1952 and they had two daughters. Dr. Lolley attended Samford University where he earned his bachelor of arts degree, and while in college pastored part time among three churches. In 1957 he graduated from Southeastern Baptist Theological Seminary with his bachelor of divinity followed by his ThM in 1958, serving in pastoral roles during each. He then attended Southwestern Baptist Theological Seminary where he earned his ThD degree in 1964. The First Baptist Church of

Winston-Salem provided his first fulltime pastoral position from 1962 until 1974.[1]

While committed to his call as a pastor, Dr. Lolley was involved in numerous other roles. In 1967 he was the president of the North Carolina Baptist Pastors' Conference, and he was also a part of the Executive Committee of the Southern Baptist Convention from 1969 to 1974. He served on a number of community boards such as the Winston-Salem Chamber of Commerce in the early 1970s.[2] His involvement demonstrated his deep care for community, which would remain central during his presidency.

Upon the retirement of Dr. Olin T. Binkley, Dr. Lolley was selected as the third president of the seminary in the spring of 1974. He began his role as president on August 1, 1974, but his official inauguration did not take place until March 11, 1976, in order to correspond with Founder's Day and the school's anniversary. He would be the first alumnus from Southeastern to serve as president and the first president who did not come directly from an academic setting.[3]

Dr. Lolley set high standards for himself as president and built an atmosphere of openness and cooperation. He emphasized unity, service, and cooperation. From the start he desired a "participatory administration," insisting that the faculty have a role in decision making for the school.[4] He helped the school develop a long-range plan which included participation of the board of trustees, faculty and staff, students, alumni, and even members of the community. He also regularly held what were known as President's Forums each month where the student body could gather and raise questions or concerns regarding seminary life.[5] Not only at the school, but also in the community, President Lolley's desire for cooperation and relationship was evident.

Dr. Lolley prioritized building relationships with the community. He and his wife regularly visited Hardee's and made themselves available for conversation with students and community members.[6] The school also held an annual New Year's lunch for the community which continued for a number of years.[7] Through this leadership, Southeastern would grow as a physical campus and as a student body.

Missions also remained of great importance to Dr. Lolley and the school. An article reflecting on Southeastern's heart for missions during this time stated that "Mission involvement—both at home and overseas—is at the heart of Southeastern Seminary."[8] Practicums in home missions and world religions were developed, allowing students training and opportunities to share the gospel. Especially significant, in fall of 1979 the Fletcher Visiting Professor of Missions was established. This provided an opportunity for the school to invite specialized scholars to instruct students on mission work.[9]

The emphasis on missions was both academic and practical. The faculty and students all remained involved with mission work both at home and abroad, with numerous alumni serving with the North American and International Mission Boards. Often professors used their sabbaticals to teach overseas or visit missionaries. Dr. Lolley himself spent a number of summers lecturing, speaking around the world, and visiting missionaries in numerous countries. In the summer of 1983, he took six weeks to visit various countries and the missions work taking place.[10] Just as with the running of the school, Dr. Lolley saw cooperation and partnership as essential for mission work.

At this time, the previous Field Work department established under Dr. Stealey was developed into a new Formation in Ministry department. The Formation in Ministry department sought to help students gain experience in ministry with assistance and mentorship.[11] Instruction encouraged participation, whether in missions, pastoring, or education. In addition to keeping education practical, accessibility of education for those actively engaged in local church ministry was also important. Evening courses were offered on campus for laypeople and Sunday School teachers and a January Bible Study Institute was held several times on campus to help train those leading Bible studies in their churches.[12]

From Southeastern's earliest years, evangelism played a foundational role and Dr. Lolley maintained this vision with the addition of an evangelism professor. For a number of years, he and members of the school worked tirelessly to promote and raise money for an evangelism professor. The importance of this position to the school was evidenced through the notable fundraising efforts put forth to endow a professorship. Finally, in June of 1978, the school appointed John W. Tresch to serve for three years as evangelism professor. When his time was complete, Dr. Delos Miles filled the position of Professor of Evangelism in 1981.[13] Evangelism would continue to be central to the curriculum and mission of Southeastern.

Though much good took place over his fourteen years as president, Dr. Lolley's presidency was not without controversy. The conservative movement of the early-1980s within the Southern Baptist Convention brought much change to the convention and its seminaries. In the midst of these events, Dr. Lolley officially offered his resignation to the board of trustees on November 17, 1987. He concluded his time as president on March 31, 1988. At the request of the newly elected president, Lewis A. Drummond, Dr. Lolley returned to lead the spring and summer graduations held in May and July 1988.[14] He would leave behind many programs, developments, and structures on which others would build.

BRASWELL AND LOLLEY

Experience with President

Lolley and I Arrive for Employment on the Same Day

Dr. Randall Lolley spoke to my Doctor of Ministry class during the fall semester of 1972. He was pastor of the First Baptist Church of Winston-Salem, North Carolina. I had never met him. He was a winsome speaker, quite folksy and practical in his insights about the churches and ministries.

After completing the Doctor of Ministry degree, our family had returned to Iran in August of 1973 expecting to serve another four-year term of missionary service. I would be teaching at the Faculty of Islamic Theology of the University of Teheran and Damavand College. Early in 1974 I received a surprising telephone call from Dr. Raymond Brown, Southeastern Seminary's Dean, which would eventually lead to my election to the faculty at Southeastern as Associate Professor of Church History and Missions.

Little did we realize that upon our return to North Carolina, President Binkley would be retired, Dean Brown would be on sabbatical leave, and there would be a new president of Southeastern Seminary.

The new president, Dr. Randall Lolley, was beginning his presidency on August 1, the same day my employment began.

President Lolley and Participatory Administration

Upon the beginning of the fall semester on August 1, 1974, President Lolley welcomed the two new professors, Dr. George Braswell and Rick Spencer, in the first chapel service to sign the Abstract of Principles document required of all elected faculty members in all six Southern Baptist seminaries.

Since Dean Brown was on sabbatical leave and would return to join the faculty as a teaching professor, there was no dean to begin the year. President Lolley advised the faculty that he desired to have "a participatory administration" which would involve the faculty in all major decisions in the life of the seminary. He suggested for the academic year 1974–1975 to name an "Academic Coordinator" to work in the dean's office until a Dean could be selected beginning the 1975 academic year.

The faculty voted on two nominees, Professor Luther Copeland and Professor John Steely, by secret ballot. President Lolley announced that the vote was a tie. Professor Copeland withdrew and President Lolley named Professor Steely as "Academic Coordinator," and stated that a search would begin for a Dean to assume office by the next academic year. This decision about the dean's office was the initiation of the president's desire to have a "participatory administration."

The Beginning of Tough Decisions

In my first meeting in his office President Lolley was most gracious. He had done a lot of homework and indicated to me that the seminary would assist me in moving expenses and that a loan up to $4,000 with 4% interest for the purchase of a house would be available through the seminary. I learned that my compensation would be set at the first stage of five for the Associate Professor level. This was in the $11,000 range and included health and retirement benefits.

When first Dean Brown had telephoned me in Teheran, he indicated that my election to the faculty would be for a three-year term and afterward consideration for tenure would depend on my completion of the PhD degree. Dean Brown also had the same kind of understanding with Rick Spencer. Professor Spencer was completing his PhD in New Testament at Emory University, and I was enrolled in the PhD program at UNC Chapel Hill in Cultural Anthropology.

President Lolley had many important matters during his early days in office. Word came somehow to Professor Spencer and me that President Lolley was considering the question of tenure for us two would be the sixth year on the faculty instead of the third year.

Somehow later Rick and I learned that several faculty members told the President it would be unfair to change a longer time for consideration for tenure than promised us upon employment. President Lolley agreed to the original understanding that consideration for tenure would come in our third year.

Lolley, Braswell, and King Henry VIII

When Dean Brown called me in Teheran to invite me to join the faculty, he told me that they wanted my title to be in Church History and Missions. I would teach Church History and Missions until a church historian could be elected to the faculty. Then my title would change to Missions and World Religions.

Professor John Steely and I taught sections of Church History for my first two years. It was a four-hour course and met an hour Tuesday through Friday. One of my sections was scheduled each day from 3 p.m. to 4 p.m. The notes I took under my Yale University Divinity School Professor, Dr. Roland Bainton, were heavily used. Dr. Bainton was a world-renowned scholar, a lively lecturer who made his subject come alive.

I decided to divide the large class into groups to research select topics in church history and to present their topic in a most interesting format to keep the class awake especially Fridays from 3 to 4 p.m. One student group chose to research the reign of Henry VIII and present it in a drama context. They dressed the parts of the times and overly stressed the relationship of the king to his wives. They had the class's attention in roaring laughter. No one went to sleep, but one student was offended and visited the President's office with his complaint.

President Lolley later approached me in the hallway outside his office, and in our conversation brought up the complaint of the student. Then with a Lolley grin he said to let him know about the presentation next time, and he would like to have a front row seat.

Intrigue between Faculty and President

The faculty was divided into four areas of administration of academic studies: Biblical (B), Theological (T), History (H), and Ministry (M). Each area had a faculty member who served a term as convener. Each area met once a month, discussed its curriculum and personnel needs, and made its monthly report to the faculty meeting.

Church History and Missions was in the H area. During my turn as area convener there was the need for providing President Lolley a name to be elected to teach church history. After many sessions of discussion with differing opinions the nominee was chosen upon a divided vote. It was my duty to report the name with the area's discussion to President Lolley. He accepted the name with approval. I was to learn later that a dissenting colleague went to the President to try to persuade him to choose his candidate. I therefore, not eager to do so, went to the President and told him we had had an open and extensive conversation about the recommendation and stood behind it.

The H area members who recommended the nominee wanted a breath of fresh air in the qualified candidate that the area recommended while the dissenting colleague wanted a friend of his acquaintance. President Lolley agreed with the area's choice, and that candidate was elected to the faculty. The President could have decided differently, but he honored the process.

Tradition had established faculty meetings to be held at 3 p.m. on Wednesdays each month. Many faculty held interim pastorates in churches some distance from the seminary which had meetings and suppers, and which necessitated driving some distances. Therefore, long-winded faculty meetings necessitated some members to leave before the meeting concluded. President Lolley desired the meetings to be moved to another afternoon. I agreed but others wanted meetings to continue on Wednesdays. And so they did. When President Patterson assumed office things changed. That change is for another telling.

Lolley, Braswell, and Soccer

I seldom missed a faculty meeting. But one time I did. I told President Lolley that I would not be present for a meeting because my son was the goalie on the Guilford College soccer team, and the team was playing Wake Forest University as an underdog on the date of the next meeting. I knew that the president loved Wake Forest University as he had been pastor of the First Baptist Church of Winston-Salem. I saw the game in Greensboro. My son had a 1 to 0 upset win stopping many goal attempts. Upon my return to campus, I saw the president. He asked me how the game turned out. I told him of the upset win. He responded that he would go with me the next time. I asked if he would cancel the faculty meeting. He grinned the Lolley grin and replied that it would be worth it.

Fletcher, Visiting Profrssor of Missions

President Lolley's placement of missions as a focus of the seminary occurred with the establishment of the Fletcher Visiting Professor of Missions. During his presidency many home and foreign missionaries came to campus for a semester, year, or summer school.

My wife, Joan, served on a committee supported by the president to raise money to furnish two missionary apartments on campus which had been appropriated by the president.

Braswell, Origin of Practicum in World Missions, and Lolley Support

President Lolley supported my teaching mission classes and in taking students on mission journeys. In planning for my first sabbatical leave I applied for a grant from the Association of Theological Schools (ATS). Upon joining the faculty from serving in Iran with the mission board, I had observed the tremendous increase of religious pluralism across the nation and the need for equipping students and churches for ministry and mission to their religious neighbors among whom were Hindus, Buddhists, Muslims, Jews, Mormons, and many others. I spoke with President Lolley about this possible proposal to ATS which would include research into world religion communities which would result in a new seminary class titled Practicum in World Religions.

The President enthusiastically supported the proposal and sent a letter of support for the grant to ATS. The proposal was accepted, and the grant was given. I spent part of the year in Washington, D.C. visiting religious communities, meeting their religious leaders, and gaining their support to bring my students for seminars in their places of education and worship. Upon completion of this research, the faculty adopted my course into the curriculum as the Practicum in World Religions. During the year of research, President Lolley made a point to call to hear about the research project.

President Lolley and I made a pact. He agreed that I could schedule the Practicum in World Religions at a time that would necessitate my being absent from spring graduation ceremonies and allowing students to take this course and still make it back in time to meet regular summer school courses if they desired. I deeply appreciated the spirit and commitment of President Lolley to his faculty colleague and to his insight and commitment to this course in missions and world religions. The practicum was offered every year with his support with dozens of students spending nine days in Washington, D.C.

Student Unwell in Israel and Lolley to the Rescue

In planning to take some 45 students in the "famous" class, Practicum in World Religions, to Israel, President Lolley indicated he would like to go with us. At the last minute he had to cancel his plans. In Israel we held seminars with Jewish, Christian, Muslim, Bahá'í, and Druze leaders from Bethlehem to Jerusalem to Haifa.

Leaving on the return flight from Tel Aviv, one of my students, a native African, began to have hallucinations and had to be restrained by my students and flight attendants until we arrived in Amsterdam. The captain called ahead to contact a Baptist missionary. Upon arrival the missionary took the distressed student for psychiatric care.

I called President Lolley who recommended leaving the student under medical care and the care of a mission until his recovery to return to the campus. The student returned to campus, later graduated, and with his family returned to his village to minister in his church. President Lolley and I learned from the student's wife that he had fasted for weeks prior to fulfilling his dream to go to the "holy land." After a week of intense class travel his mind and body were exhausted. Sadly, he later died in his village from a snake bite.

Lolley Sends Us to Meet
with President Jimmy Carter

President Lolley requested that another professor and I meet him in his office. He explained an invitation he had received from the White House of President Jimmy Carter to send two seminary representatives to Washington, D.C. to be a part of a discussion on the Panama Canal Treaty. He asked us to attend. We flew to Washington. First there was a meeting in a large conference room in a hotel in which state department officials gave background on the treaty. Then some several hundred attendees were bused over to the White House to hear President Carter's remarks.

My first book, *To Ride A Magic Carpet*, had been published by Broadman Press. The editors sent a copy of the book to President Carter because of its background on Iran and because Iran was emerging as a key player on the international stage. Mrs. Carter sent a thank you note to the editors on behalf of the President. I took a copy of my book hoping that President Carter would sign it. But to my chagrin I stood in the third line in the roped area inside the White House where the President spoke to us. As he passed by, I held the book high above my head and like a child called out, "Mr. President, were you able to read my book on Iran?" He looked toward me, smiled, and walked on down the roped aisle. (See the Mrs. Jimmy Carter letter in Braswell archives.)

Upon our return to campus, we reported to President Lolley about our Washington visit. With the characteristic

Lolley wit he asked me why I did not fly on my magic carpet over the ropes to the president.

Lolley Support of My Sabbaticals to Taiwan and across the USA

On another sabbatical leave I accepted an invitation from Dr. Sam James of the International Mission Board to write up a church growth proposal for the missionaries and the national Baptist leaders of Taiwan, and to spend the appropriate time with the church leaders across the island during the fall semester to implement it.

Also, on another sabbatical I accepted an invitation from the North American Mission Board to survey the presence of Islam and Muslims across the United States. After the visits with many Muslim communities, I proposed a weekend meeting at Pepperdine University in Los Angeles with assigned identical topics for eight Muslims and eight Baptists to present.

I always met with President Lolley to discuss the sabbatical projects. He was enthusiastic about the projects and wished he could drop in on both. I asked him if he would like to be one of the Baptists for the dialogue meeting in Los Angeles. He agreed. I told him I would get back to him in the spring with more details about the subject and the time in May. But his schedule could not be worked out.

Lolley and My Determination to Get a Professor of Evangelism

I always found President Lolley's mind and heart and soul were attuned to missions and evangelism both in the seminary curriculum, in the life of the churches, and in both home and foreign missions and missionaries. When I joined the faculty there was little presence of any mission and evangelism courses. President Lolley worked diligently to include a professor of evangelism on the faculty. I remember when he discussed his idea in a faculty meeting several faculty spoke out that every faculty member was an evangelist in his classes, meaning that no professor of evangelism was needed at Southeastern.

President Lolley did not give up. I was invited to be Missionary Day speaker at Midwestern Baptist Theological Seminary in Kansas City, Missouri. Dr. Delos Miles, Professor of Evangelism, introduced me in the chapel service. Later President Lolley invited Dr. Miles to be the first full-time elected faculty member in evangelism.

Professors Philbeck, Balentine, and Ashcraft from Midwestern Baptist Seminary also joined the Southeastern faculty.

Conflict Resolution and the President

During a meeting of the H area to discuss my sabbatical proposal in relation to the invitations of both the International and North American Mission Boards, I initiated discussion about who might be brought on campus for my year away to teach the courses in missions and world religions.

I spoke of former Southeastern professor Dr. Luther Copeland. Dr. and Mrs. Copeland were SBC missionaries to Japan when President Stealey invited Dr. Copeland to be Professor of Missions and World Religions in the 1950s. Dr. Copeland was my faculty colleague when I joined the faculty in 1974.

After our two-year colleagueship Dr. and Mrs. Copeland responded to the invitation of the Japan Baptist Convention to become chancellor at Seinan Gakuin University. What an honor for the Japanese Baptists to invite a non-Japanese to such a post! But the Copelands were now retiring and coming to live in Raleigh. He had taught nineteen years at Southeastern before returning to Japan.

So I suggested that Dr. Luther Copeland be invited to be the Fletcher Visiting Professor of Missions to teach the courses in missions and world religions during my sabbatical leave. The H area members agreed—all but one. But the positive response to send Dr. Copeland's name to President Lolley persisted and his name was sent to the president.

Later President Lolley met with me for further discussion about Dr. Copeland and told me another H area faculty member had approached him to register his dissatisfaction. I must admit that I was near anger and certainly not pleased. Both the president and I knew that the same member had voiced his opposition earlier in the search for a church history professor. President Lolley proceeded to invite Dr. Copeland and the esteemed professor was well accepted in teaching missions and world religions.

Gift from the President of a Blue Carolina Coat

One Christmas season a knock came on our front door on historic North Main Street. It was President Lolley. We invited him in for a cup of hot tea sitting around Persian carpets from Iran. He had draped over his arm a dry cleaner pressed Carolina blue sports coat. He had picked it up somewhere, thought about me and my studies at Chapel Hill in cultural anthropology and was presenting it to me.

I told him I deeply appreciated the gift knowing his great fondness for the hoped for victories of the Demon Deacons over the Tar Heels in all sports. He had read my first published book on Iran, *To Ride A Magic Carpet*, which described our family's missionary service in Iran. I reminded him of my very first visits to the Magi in Teheran and told him he came to our home bearing a gift which was most thoughtful.

Later, President Lolley asked me to represent the seminary at the inauguration of Dr. C. D. Spangler as Chancellor of the University of North Carolina at Chapel Hill.

Coffee at Hardee's with Townfolks

President Lolley was a people person and a pastor at heart. Many remembrances of him were shared by townspeople. He, and sometimes Lou with him, so very often would drop by Hardee's downtown and drink coffee with the locals. Every New Year he would ask professors to join in serving townspeople and strangers the traditional meal in the seminary cafeteria. They never forgot the seminary president and his faculty families.

Paschal Golf Course and Arnold Palmer

President Lolley did not hesitate to involve the faculty in his "participatory administration." He asked me to represent the seminary on the Board of Directors of Paschal Golf Course. The seminary inherited the course in the properties gained when Wake Forest College moved to Winston-Salem. The Board independently operated the club by paying the seminary one dollar a year. Local town business folk were elected by board members for terms of service.

I served for eleven years. Paschal Golf Club is a nine-hole course on which the famous Arnold Palmer practiced when a student at the college. The Board had many challenges competing with the several eighteen-hole courses nearby. One cold winter our finances were so low we directors paid our club fees two years in advance. I went to President Lolley and told him that he got me into this "mess" and we were in trouble. He found $5,000 to give the board for survival. That was Randall Lolley.

Later the town declared Arnold Palmer Day. Mr. Palmer flew his own private jet to RDU. He was picked up and brought straight to the seminary. It was my privilege to drive him around the campus in a golf cart from Paschal. For thirty minutes we rode around, paused at Stealey Hall, Binkley Chapel, and buildings in which he had classes.

Mr. Palmer remembered the professors' names, some of whom I had as a college student. As we concluded our tour, I asked him if he could sign nine Paschal Golf Club score cards to give the Board of Directors and my sons who were golfers. He said it would be his pleasure. Mr. Palmer, celebrity that he was, had all the time in the world to talk with me for thirty minutes in a golf cart and sign slowly, while talking, all the score cards.

President Lolley had laid the groundwork for this experience years before by asking me to represent the seminary at Paschal.

The President's Affirmation of
Dr. Brevard Childs as Lecturer

Dr. Brevard Childs was my Professor of Old Testament at Yale University Divinity School. During my chairmanship of the Lecture Committee, I suggested that Dr. Childs be invited to give the two lectures of the Spring Lectureship. President Lolley was enthusiastic of issuing the invitation. During his campus visit Joan prepared a delicious Iranian meal and invited Dr. Childs and President and Mrs. Lolley and members of the Old Testament faculty.

The President and Faculty Salaries

Faculty salaries were unknown with respect to any public knowledge. What was known was there were five steps in the assistant professor category; five steps in the associate professor category; and there were ten steps in the full professor category. There was no public information as to attaining these ranks except once elected originally to the faculty at whatever entry step a faculty member progressed each year to a higher step and received some increase in pay if any. For example, I was elected to the second step of associate professor with corresponding salary and retirement and health benefits.

Some faculty members approached the president about the low faculty salaries. President Lolley said he would look into the matter and call a special faculty meeting to present his findings. An older faculty member who was at the top scale of full professor and my close friend came to me with an idea. He surmised that the president would reward salary increases to his former professors who had taught him at Southeastern and lesser increases for others. He asked my opinion. I told him I favored a salary scale that certainly honored the older faculty but also should be based on professional merit of research and writing as well as in class teaching and relationships to students and churches.

My close colleague suggested that he, the older at the top of the faculty salary and I, the younger faculty member, go talk with the president. In our conversation with President Lolley, we politely expressed our views and concerns. He listened and said he would make a report to a special faculty meeting.

At the special meeting with all faculty eagerly awaiting his report we learned that the top of the scale professors were given significant increases compared to those on the lower scales. It appeared that longevity and some kind of loyalty were rewarded.

Later I learned that two older professors went to the president on my behalf to tell him that it was a real possibility that another school would lure me away if the pay scale was not adjusted for the younger faculty. The president adjusted my scale to full professor with salary increase. One of the professors who went to bat for me shared his letter to the president with me much later. It is in my seminary archives. Perhaps other younger faculty received similar support from colleagues.

Christian Missions Class Asks about Salaries

In my Christian Missions class, we were discussing the history and programs of the foreign and home mission boards. A student asked about the salary of missionaries and those of the board personnel. I replied that a missionary salary was based on the number of children and the economical living index of the specific country of service. It did not matter whether one was a medical doctor or a professor or a schoolteacher. I told the class I would inquire about the salary of the president of the International Mission Board.

Upon inquiry I received no answer. I then asked the class if they would support the proposal of equal pay for all SBC board leaders and missionaries and pastors with the caveat of supplementing number of children and living index. In a class of sixty, one student affirmatively raised his hand. I later told President Lolley this class happening. He smiled and replied that it was a matter worthy of study.

Storms Brewing, Dr. Stanley,
Peace Committee, and Lolley's Counsel

Beginning in the early 1980s, storms were brewing within the Southern Baptist Convention especially about the administrations and faculties of the seminaries as to their teachings. Dr. Charles Stanley was elected president of the convention and a Peace Committee was formed to visit each seminary and report back to the convention their findings.

At a faculty meeting President Lolley polled the faculty as to their view of his inviting Dr. Stanley to speak in chapel. He reminded the faculty that seminary tradition was to invite each new president of the convention to visit the campus and speak in chapel. Only two faculty members voiced a positive response for the president to invite Dr. Stanley.

One was myself.

President Lolley made the decision to invite Dr. Stanley to speak in chapel and to meet with the faculty over lunch in the meeting room of the seminary cafeteria. After chapel I went to the cafeteria to find Dr. Stanley waiting in the room alone. I introduced myself, proceeded to take him through the food line, and sit beside him for lunch as members of the faculty came in. I told him that I had been pastor of the Cullowhee Baptist Church at Western Carolina University near Fruitland Bible Institute where he had served as pastor and teacher. There was very little response from him.

After lunch President Lolley recognized Dr. Stanley to speak. In his remarks Dr. Stanley suggested that he would like to meet faculty in their offices for a more leisurely conversation. The meeting went downhill after his suggestion. I think faculty members already felt discomfort being present in the meeting with all the previous news that they were under suspicion as some heretics. And Dr. Stanley's words offered no encouragement of goodly fellowship. So the meeting was adjourned.

President Lolley announced that he would like to visit each faculty member in the faculty member's office to converse about the upcoming meeting with the Peace Committee. He came to my corner office on the third floor of Stealey Hall. One window looked out on the water fountain and the other toward the library. How fitting, I thought, in troubled times: a soothing water fountain and a library filled with wisdom of the ages for these times.

The president counseled me to continue my classroom teaching and research and writing and my interim pastorate. He said he would meet with the peace committee and for me not to have any worries. I told him that my classes were open to visitors, that my writings were available for any to read, and that I would carry out my responsibilities as usual. With that he slapped me on the back and departed in good spirits.

The peace committee requested Dr. Lolley to solicit from a few faculty clarifications from their lectures and writings. He did so and forwarded the information to the committee. The committee again asked certain faculty to clarify further some of their requests which they did. I was never asked and had indicated to the president my openness for any to speak with me.

The Beginning of the End
of the Lolley Administration:
Déjà Vu for Me

The fall semester 1987 began my sabbatical leave for the fall and spring semesters. I was preparing to depart for Taiwan for a church growth project when the fall convocation was held in Binkley Chapel. I did not attend the convocation and Dean Ashcraft came by our house to tell me that I had been awarded the Faculty in Excellence in Teaching Award. He also extended the congratulations of President Lolley.

Little did I realize that upon my return from sabbatical leave at the end of summer 1988, President Lolley and Dean Ashcraft would have resigned their positions and the trustees would have elected Lewis Drummond as president. And that Professor Bob Dale would be acting dean until a Dean could be selected.

Here we go again! The same events were occurring when I joined the faculty in 1974. President Binkley and Dean Brown who had invited me to join the faculty were gone, and Dr. Randall Lolley was the new president, and there was no dean in the office.

I had been away on sabbatical leave for a most productive time of research and writing, and at the same time there was tumult on campus and among the faculty, students, trustees, and alumni and across the Southern Baptist Convention.

My Later Contacts with President and Mrs. Lolley

I do not recall seeing President Lolley again until he and Lou retired into The Cypress in Raleigh. I was invited many times to speak to the residents of The Cypress on subjects about Iran, the Middle East, and world religions. I also took the residents to Hindu and Buddhist temples, synagogues, mosques, and Mormon churches for seminars. Dr. Lolley would always introduce me when I spoke at The Cypress. He always praised my teaching and writing and how much he respected my ministry. Afterward Joan and I would visit with them over a meal and remember about the good times at Southeastern. I do not recall any conversation about the controversy.

Dr. Lolley held at least three interim pastorates during his early days in retirement at The Cypress. He invited me to speak at each one for a Wednesday night series on Iran, the Middle East, and associated topics. Again, we would eat together and talk about our good times together.

In his latter days he was confined to the medical unit of The Cypress. In my last visit with him, Lou and I held his hand and talked as he listened and smiled. President Lolley was my good president. He had a heart for missions and supported my work, reaching from Washington all the way to Israel. Personally, he always affirmed me in my Christian pilgrimage and ministry and mission on campus in the classroom and in my travels to missionaries around the globe.

8

PRESIDENT
LEWIS A. DRUMMOND
1988-1992

A BRIEF HISTORY

Following the service of President Randall Lolley, Dr. Lewis A. Drummond was selected to fill the role of president at Southeastern Seminary. Though his presidency would be brief, he would set a vision for the seminary that would help shape its entire future.

Dr. Lewis Addison Drummond grew up in Dixon, Illinois, and as a young man served in the military where he was baptized by a chaplain while in Japan. He earned his bachelor's degree in English from Samford University in 1950, and while there he committed to enter the ministry. He and Betty Rae Love were married in 1950. He then went to Southwestern Baptist Theological Seminary in Fort Worth, Texas, where he received a bachelor of divinity in New Testament in 1955 and a ThM in Philosophy in 1958. He would go on to earn his PhD at King's College,

University of London, in England in 1963.[1] Dr. Drummond pastored for a number of years in Alabama, Texas, and Kentucky, and then took a position at Spurgeon's College in London from 1968 until 1973 where he served as the first full-time professor of evangelism in Europe and held the school's chair of evangelism.[2]

Dr. Drummond's work was colored by his great passion for evangelism. In addition to serving as an associate evangelist with the Billy Graham Evangelistic Team during crusades in Australia and Poland, Dr. Drummond began teaching as the Billy Graham Professor of Evangelism at Southern Baptist Theological Seminary in Louisville, Kentucky, in 1973. In 1981 he became the administrative director at the Billy Graham Center of Evangelism. He was also on the Committee on Evangelism and Education with the Baptist World Alliance when the committee began in 1975.[3] During this time, he was a proficient writer and published several works. Dr. Drummond's heart for evangelism would not only direct his own career but would eventually influence the direction of Southeastern Seminary.

In 1988, Southeastern elected Dr. Drummond to the presidency on March 14, and he officially took office on April 1. Dr. Billy Graham spoke at his inauguration on October 11, 1988. In his address at the inauguration, Dr. Drummond stated that "our seminary will be proud to graduate students who will seek to fulfill the Great Commission of the Lord Jesus Christ."[4] With these words, Dr. Drummond, bringing his passion for and experience in evangelism, centered the work of the seminary on the Great Commission which could be seen threaded throughout Southeastern's past and now at the very heart of the school.

The direction of education during Dr. Drummond's presidency took the foundation of evangelism and world missions that had already been established and propelled it forward. President Drummond stressed evangelism through his writings, speaking opportunities, and focus on what would eventually become the Center for Great Commission Studies. In 1989 he expressed his vision for this center by writing, "It is what I have been calling of late my 'Big Dream'...I have challenged us to inaugurate a full 'school,' or 'center' of world missions, evangelism, and church-growth."[5] He desired that the center provide resources and training for students to grow in the practice of evangelism and missions. It would officially be launched in the spring of 1991.[6]

Southeastern Baptist Theological Seminary put this evangelistic vision into practice. Students and staff traveled to other parts of the country and world for evangelism and missions. Especially significant during these years was activity in Eastern Europe. Students and professors engaged in evangelistic work in Czechoslovakia and Romania, even forming a partnership with a Bible institute in Romania.[7]

Along with these noteworthy goals for the seminary, President Drummond also recognized that a primary focus of his attention would have to be seeking peace and harmony at the school.[8] The fresh challenges of controversy left noticeable division at the seminary, and Dr. Drummond attempted to bring some level of restoration.

In addition to this challenge, Dr. Drummond had to face the pressure of accreditation issues with the Southern Association of Colleges and Schools and the Association of Theological Schools. Both agencies had concerns regarding some of the school's policies and procedures. Dr. Drummond and the administration worked hard to meet requirements, but the school would eventually be placed on probation by both agencies. Accreditation would not be restored until the following president took office.[9] However, Dr. Drummond helped establish a new faculty selection process to begin addressing the agencies' concerns.[10]

Dr. Drummond not only experienced institution-related challenges in his presidency but also with his personal health. In fall of 1989, in just over a year as president, Dr. Drummond received treatments for cancer and in December 1989 underwent surgery. Though challenging, after these treatments he was able to return to work by January 1990.[11]

After serving as president of the seminary for four years, Dr. Drummond announced his retirement to the trustees in 1992 and finished his duties in June of that year.[12] He would then join Beeson Divinity School at Samford University.[13] Dr. Drummond's time as president of Southeastern left a legacy of evangelism and a heart for world missions through the Center for Great Commission Studies that would take root and flourish in the coming years.

BRASWELL
AND DRUMMOND

Experience with President

Déjà Vu: from Lolley to Drummond

Upon my return from sabbatical leave, it was déjà vu all over again. I joined the faculty upon the invitation of President Binkley and Dean Brown. When I arrived from Iran the president had retired and the dean was on sabbatical leave, all unknown to me when accepting the teaching position. Now as I returned for the fall semester in 1988, Dr. Lewis Drummond had been elected president and there was no dean.

Turmoil and conflict had ravaged the campus during 1987–1988. President Lolley and Dean Ashcraft and three vice presidents had resigned. Faculty members had left, retired, or were contemplating retiring or leaving. Enrollment was down and finances were threatened.

President Drummond was known throughout the world of evangelism as an outstanding preacher and writer. He was a close friend of the Reverend Billy Graham. He came to Southeastern from serving as Director of the Billy Graham School of Evangelism at the Southern Baptist Theological Seminary. The trustees elected him president hoping he could bring a peaceful transition to the campus.

Controversy over Selection of Dean

An early crisis focused on the election of a new dean. First, the president solicited nominees from the faculty while submitting his own nominee Professor Russ Bush who was on the faculty of Southwestern Baptist Theological Seminary. After several faculty meetings and voting on nominees, the president asked the faculty to vote on Dr. Bush. All faculty votes were against Bush. Nevertheless, President Drummond, together with the Board of Trustees, named Dr. Bush as Dean of the Faculty.

Drummond Asked Me to Speak at Alumni Meetings

President Drummond brought in as Vice President for Development and Alumni Relations Dr. George Worrell from his post as Director of Evangelism for the Oklahoma Baptist Convention.

President Drummond and Dr. Worrell urged me to speak at seminary alumni meetings held in the fall in various states. At first I refused. I figured that the alumni who attended the meetings would be divisive on their support for the happenings in the transition on campus. Since I had no plans to seek employment elsewhere, I agreed to go and speak on missions and church planting which I had emphasized in my courses for nearly twenty years.

At the luncheon meeting with the alumni of Virginia I spoke of the students planting churches across the nation and of the students going into multiple world religion communities with me to learn and to share. At the time of discussion, it was evident that the alumni were divided and conflicted over the happenings at the seminary.

I reported to President Drummond that not only was there unhappiness but hostility among the alumni about the happenings at the seminary. I encountered the same at an alumni luncheon in South Carolina.

At the annual alumni meeting held in the seminary cafeteria I, with several other faculty, were asked to speak along with President Drummond and Dr. Worrell. There were less than twenty present where in the past there would be several hundred. The discussion time was short but friendly. From these meetings and other indications, I felt the seminary was facing very difficult times.

President's Treatment for Cancer and Braswell's Conversation with Dean Bush

The faculty workshop was held a week before the fall semester began. It was my time to serve as faculty pro temp to preside over the faculty meeting in the absence of the president.

As I arrived in Broyhill Hall for the workshop Dean Russ Bush pulled me aside to tell me President Drummond was in Duke Hospital in treatment for cancer. I was to preside over the meeting with him by my side. At the conclusion of the meeting the faculty requested that I represent them and asked if Dean Bush and I would visit President Drummond to pray with him. Dean Bush and I traveled to

Duke Hospital and prayed in the President's room while Mrs. Drummond was there.

Upon returning to the campus, I told Dean Bush that I supposed he knew that the entire faculty had voted against the president's recommendation of him as dean. He acknowledged that he did. Then I told him at that time I had no intention of leaving my teaching post, that I loved all facets of my ministry and mission there, and that I would assist the seminary in ways that I could. He did not know of offers to me for other teaching positions. In all our relationships Russ Bush and I had a friendship and a colleagueship that was positive.

Unusual Called Faculty Meeting in Summer

A surprise awaited the faculty when President Drummond called an unheard-of faculty meeting in the summer. What could be so urgent it could not wait until the upcoming faculty workshop?

The faculty gathered in the small chapel. I wondered if we were gathering for a funeral. The President led us in prayer and then swiftly turned the meeting over to the Vice President of Business, Mr. Paul Fletcher. In short Mr. Fletcher, a holdover from the Lolley administration, informed us that the finances of the seminary were in a very critical state. Then Dean Bush told us that the status and prospects of institutional money flow for the fall and spring semesters were such that even those with tenure might be affected as to their faculty appointments.

Beginning of the End: Faculty Opting Out

We left the meeting wondering why all this suddenness and negative view about finances and their implications upon all seminary employees. In the immediate days ahead, it seemed faculty members, one by one, went to President Drummond's office for private conferences.

One faculty colleague returning from sabbatical leave discussed with me his uncertainty about staying at the seminary. Although he just returned from sabbatical leave, and tradition was that one stayed at least another year to teach, I told him to go to the president's office right away. He did just that and a "deal" was worked out for him to depart.

Drummond's Own Challenges

President Drummond in accepting the trustees' offer of the seminary presidency had his own considerations upon his acceptance. Later strife developed over the amount of money spent in the renovation and furnishing of the president's house on campus.

There was uneasiness that his travel budget included Mrs. Drummond. There was concern over the granting of his membership in the Capital Club of Raleigh for entertaining guests at seminary expense. There was great chagrin over his lack of skills in administration of the seminary.

From my viewpoint and from my relations with President Drummond he was a kind and considerate gentleman who was serving beyond his talents as the administrator of

Southeastern Baptist Theological Seminary. In the turbulence and great chaos at the seminary which he inherited from day one, and in his deteriorated and ever-present deteriorating relations with the faculty, trustees, and many alumni and students, there was really no positive outcome for the future of his presidency.

He and Dean Bush had asked me to serve on the long-range planning committee with trustee, administrative, alumni, and student representation. We met at the president's home periodically. But enrollment decline and negative finances continued to hound any future developments.

The Alliance of Baptists, the Baptist Seminary in Richmond, the Cooperative Baptist Fellowship, and other assumed names of "Moderate Baptists" were on the horizon for development. Words and thoughts were expressed by others outside the seminary that Southeastern Seminary would become an indoctrination school and would be surpassed by the new entities.

Approach to Me of an Endowed Chair

It was about this time that I was approached by another seminary for consideration for an endowed chair, and I had the conversation with former president Dr. Binkley in his home about which I have already written. It was also about this time that the name of Dr. Paige Patterson was publicized to be named the next president of Southeastern Seminary.

And so President Drummond left the seminary to join the faculty of Samford University. He would return to his roots in evangelism. It reminded me of the address of the Reverend Billy Graham at Dr. Drummond's seminary inauguration praising him as a great evangelist. He was comfortable returning to his true roots.

9

PRESIDENT
L. PAIGE PATTERSON
1992-2003

A BRIEF HISTORY

The year 1992 saw the announcement of Dr. Paige Patterson as the newest president of Southeastern Seminary. Facing a number of challenges, Dr. Patterson focused his attention on strengthening the school academically and growing its faculty and student body and pushed it forward in a worldwide mission.

Dr. Paige Patterson was born Leighton Paige Patterson in October 1942, in Fort Worth, Texas. His father, Thomas Armour Patterson, was a pastor and part of the Baptist General Convention of Texas for a number of years as the executive director.[1] Dr. Patterson accepted Christ at the age of nine and, feeling called into ministry, was given the opportunity to preach for the first time in his early teens. These early chances at preaching would lead to a lifetime of pastoring. In addition to an early start in preaching, Dr.

Patterson also traveled to a number of different countries in his teenage years. These travels opened his eyes to the needs of the world and sparked a heart for missions.[2] These foundational experiences would establish lifelong passions for preaching and worldwide evangelism which would in turn influence Southeastern Seminary.

Dr. Patterson attended Hardin-Simmons College, earning his bachelor's degree in 1965. During that time, he met and married Dorothy Jean Kelley from San Antonio, Texas. Together they would raise two children. He and Mrs. Patterson both attended New Orleans Baptist Theological Seminary where he earned his ThM in 1968 and his doctorate in 1973. He served in a number of churches including First Baptist Church, Dallas, Texas, and from 1975 until his election at Southeastern was the president of Criswell College in Dallas, Texas. During these years, he served on numerous boards, including as a trustee on the International Mission Board from 1988 until 1992, and remained involved with the Southern Baptist Convention.[3]

In May of 1992, Dr. Patterson was elected as president of Southeastern Seminary and officially began his role as president on June 15, 1992. He inherited many pressing tasks from his predecessor including accreditation issues, low enrollment, and financial struggles.[4]

Though there were challenges to be addressed, Dr. Patterson also sought to develop new areas of the school. He established and redesigned a number of programs at Southeastern in order to strengthen and deepen its academic presence. During his presidency the Doctor of Ministry program was reconstructed, and the Master of Divinity was modified with requirements in biblical languages and an increased focus on expository preaching, a focus of particular importance to Dr. Patterson. Additionally, Southeastern established its Doctor of Philosophy program. Numerous new tracks of study were introduced including one in Biblical Counseling. Especially significant was the establishment in 1995 of Southeastern's college program, which would be known as the College at Southeastern.[5]

A particularly noteworthy degree program developed in 1995—the International Church Planting degree. This was also known as the two-plus-two program. Through partnership with the International Mission Board, students completed two years of study at Southeastern followed by two years of training and work on the mission field especially focused on church planting. Following the good results from this first program, the seminary soon began a similar degree for North American church planting in partnership with the North American Mission Board.[6] In addition to representing the growth of the seminary's academic offerings, these degrees also highlighted the continued emphasis on missions and partnerships to help equip students.

Along with the church planting degrees, various other partnerships were cultivated locally and around the world. Church planting partnerships existed in New Hampshire and connections with work in Eastern Europe remained a point of focus.[7] These, and many other efforts, demonstrated the central focus of evangelism and mission work at Southeastern. Not only did Dr. Patterson encourage these endeavors toward missions and evangelism, he also participated in them himself. He and Mrs. Patterson would regularly travel around the world, often visiting students and speaking at conferences in different countries.[8]

Much was accomplished during Dr. Patterson's time as president of the seminary. Accreditation was restored and enrollment reached all-time highs.[9] Due to the growth of the student population, facilities needed renovating and more housing had to be built which led to improvements across the campus. In keeping with the focus of the school's mission, the Bailey Smith Chair of Evangelism was created in 1994.[10] Furthermore, Dr. Patterson continued the vision cast by Dr. Drummond. The Center for Great Commission Studies continued to develop and eventually obtained a permanent facility specially constructed to house the department. This building bridged the passion for missions and evangelism of Southeastern's previous president, Dr. Drummond, with Dr. Patterson's own long-held passion for worldwide missions.[11] New partnerships, degrees, and programs flourished from this center.

While Dr. Patterson was president of Southeastern, he stayed involved with Southern Baptist life and was elected as the president of the Southern Baptist Convention in 1998 and again in 1999.[12] After serving at Southeastern for eleven years, on June 24, 2003, Dr. Patterson shared that he would be taking the position as president of Southwestern Baptist Theological Seminary.[13] As president at Southeastern, he helped build numerous programs and reinforced missions and academics.

Braswell and Patterson

Experience with President

A Surprise Meeting with Dr. Patterson in My Office

I was in my office on the third floor of Stealey Hall on a sunny day in May 1992. It was a corner office with one window view of the library and the other window view of the beautiful water fountain in front of Stealey Hall.

There was a knock on the door and Dean Russ Bush entered with a red-haired man I had never met. He introduced Dr. Paige Patterson and said that Dr. Patterson had wanted to meet me. I was utterly shocked. Dean Bush left him with me.

I had often met with Ayatollahs in Iran and heard them preach in mosques. I had been a guest in their homes for meals and had drunk tea with them. I thought I could handle this meeting but wondered why me? I was puzzled that Dr. Patterson had wanted to visit with me.

He said he had read my book on my missionary experience in Iran, *To Ride A Magic Carpet*. I thought he had read some heresy in it. He was very pleasant in his conversation. He told me that he had an informally adopted brother who was Arab. He was appreciative of my background in Iran and in my missionary experience. He then said that he heard that I played tennis and asked if I would play doubles with him. I thought that was strange.

Then, even stranger, he told me that I would like the professors he was bringing with him from Criswell College.

In all his conversation with me it sounded like he had already been elected seminary president. After thirty minutes Dean Bush returned to retrieve him. As he was departing, he once again asked if I would play tennis with him. I told him I had played third base on the Wake Forest College baseball team, known as the hot corner, on this very campus, and asked him if he were willing to be beaten by an old baseball player? He replied that it's a deal.

Later in the afternoon Dr. Patterson met with the faculty with Dean Bush presiding. After the faculty meeting, he met with the Board of Trustees and was elected president of Southeastern Seminary.

President Patterson Requests that I Serve as Director of Doctor of Ministry Program

The situation at Southeastern seemingly did not appear well. Many faculty had departed. Enrollment was low. Finances were negative. Publicity about Southeastern was divided. Those who opposed the board of trustee action in causing President Lolley to resign, and electing Dr. Patterson as president, were voicing the demise of the seminary to a fundamentalist indoctrination school. They were forming their own theological schools and church organizations. Those who supported the election of President Patterson were positive about the change and forecast a resurgence in student enrollment and finances and especially a more vigorous program in evangelism and missions.

Dean Russ Bush approached me with the urgent invitation on behalf of President Patterson that I become the director of the Doctor of Ministry program. I told him thanks but no thanks. The next day he came back to me with the plea from the president to accept it. I talked to Joan about it. Her counsel was that I had studied for the Doctor of Ministry degree and that I had the PhD degree and had the background to do it.

I told President Patterson I would accept it on the following conditions: suspension of any applications for the year, toughen up all entrance requirements, revamp the entire curriculum, place a three-year deadline on completion of the thesis and graduation, and submit the revised program the following spring for faculty consideration. In my thinking the seminary would not become an "indoctrination school" as forecast by its critics.

President Patterson immediately accepted the proposal and offered any assistance needed in accomplishing it. Little did I know that I would serve some ten years as director and that multiple students would be enrolled at the time of my departure.

Patterson and Braswell Launch
Unique Doctoral Program in the Philippines

When the president takes the initiative to come to your office rather than ask you to come to his, you know he is up to something. President Patterson told me of his friend who was pastor of a large church in Manila, Philippines. He said, "How would you like to direct a Doctor of Ministry degree program for select Philippine pastors?" Upon further conversations the president agreed with my proposal to admit qualified pastors with all the requirements of the present program with no exceptions including graduation in three years. Period!

During the three years, twelve pastors met all entrance requirements, accomplished all required studies, and graduated on time. I, along with select faculty, offered classes in Manila. President Patterson supported the twelve pastors coming to Wake Forest for a summer school to meet residence requirements. Graduation exercises were held in the large church in Manila with President Patterson, Dean Bush, Registrar Alexander, me, and the students and their families gathered from as far away as the island of Cebu.

Mission accomplished! It is an example of a president's vision and a faculty readiness to do the hard work of accomplishing it.

President and Mrs. Patterson, Braswell, and Wake Forest Baptist Church

Shortly after the Pattersons moved into the president's house, they sent a letter to the pastor of Wake Forest Baptist Church requesting, not membership, but watchcare. They stated they would leave their membership at the First Baptist Church of Dallas for a time. The pastor presented their request to the meeting of the deacons of which I was a part. It was not a favorable discussion and decision to affirm the request.

I asked the deacons to have the pastor arrange a meeting of them with us so we could tell them of the life of the church, its leadership, its underlying beliefs and practices, with the assumption that the Pattersons might see that another church might be preferable. My suggestion was not acceptable. Then I proposed that the pastor compose and send a letter to them stating that it was best not to pursue watchcare.

Mrs. Patterson telephoned me the next night asking if I could meet with them in the president's office the next morning. They had read the pastor's letter and asked my opinion. I told them that I felt the church as a whole would reject their request for watchcare. They asked to pray and afterward I left. They later withdrew their request. President Patterson never raised the concern again.

President and Professor "Battle" over Moving to a New Office and Dr. Solc

On another occasion President Patterson took the initiative to come to my office. With excitement in his voice, he told me he wanted to bring Dr. Josef Solc to join the faculty in evangelism and missions. Dr. Solc came from a family of pastors in the Czech Republic, had played ice hockey and tennis on the national stage, had run into difficulty as a Christian at the communist takeover, and had come to Oral Roberts University and made all American twice in tennis. He held a PhD from Southwestern Seminary and was pastor of a thriving church in Fort Worth, Texas.

I said what a blessing it would be to have him on the faculty. I also said I would welcome him to be my partner on the tennis court. The president said that he agreed. Dr. Solc became a close friend and a tennis partner who, in doubles, always protected my back.

When the Jacumin-Simpson building was completed to house faculty offices and the Center for Great Commission Studies, President Patterson spoke with me about my selecting the first faculty office in the new building. I thanked him but said my office in Stealey was full of some twenty years of books and filing cabinets and mission items and that I had rather him give it to another professor. He kept insisting and proposed that I could move to the new office and have the old office for storage and a hide out for future writing.

In my hesitancy to move, President Patterson responded to my request that Dr. Josef Solc move to the adjacent office which he did. I chose the second-floor corner office with one window viewing Wake Forest Baptist Church and the other viewing Binkley Chapel and Stealey Hall. I kept the office until my retirement.

President Requested My Mentoring of a New PhD Student

On another occasion President Patterson approached me, again in my office, telling me about a South African diplomat who he wanted to join our community as a PhD candidate and asked if I would be his mentor. Ant Greenham had worked in South African consulates in Israel and Jordan. I enthusiastically agreed. I mentored Mr. Greenham in his PhD studies.

During his research, he traveled to Jordan as I did when I taught our seminary students in the two-plus-two mission program. He and Eva, his wife, crossed the Allenby Bridge into Israel to do original research among former Arab Muslim men and women who had become Christians. This research was included in his dissertation. While in Amman Mr. Greenham and I were invited to a well-known Jordanian cabinet member's home for a meal and conversations. Mr. Greenham had established a friendship with him when he was a diplomat in Jordan.

Dr. Greenham gained his PhD, and when I retired, he became the lead professor in missions and continued teaching the Practicum in World Religions I had created in 1982.

President's Vision for Building

The long-range planning committee which President Drummond began was continued by President Patterson. We met at Magnolia Hill as called by the president. The meetings contributed to the future renovation of Mackie Hall into faculty offices, to renovations in the dormitory buildings, and to the construction of the Jacumin-Simpson building. At one meeting President Patterson said to me that he would be willing to make a significant offer to purchase Wake Forest Baptist Church for the building of a center for preaching. I did not pursue the conversation further.

My Privilege in Mentoring Students

As I directed the Doctor of Ministry program, I would oc-casionally mentor a student who requested it of me. I men-tored a missionary serving with the International Mission Board whose thesis became a published book impacting the Christian mission to the Muslim world. Another pas-tor-student became president of the Baptist State Conven-tion. A female student, who left her medical profession to enroll in the Master of Divinity program, later asked me to chair her Doctor of Ministry committee. She graduated and was hooded at graduation services by President Pat-terson and me.

President Patterson's
Heart and Support of Missions

One of President Patterson's greatest passions was to carry the gospel to the nations. The two-plus-two program was a favorite of his. A student would enroll in the basic courses on campus for two years. The next two years the student would serve in a global mission context with supervision by IMB missionaries and various faculty members would travel to their mission fields to offer classes. After four years the student would graduate, and if the student felt the calling to missionary service, then appointment could proceed.

President's Support for My Teaching in Kenya, Singapore, Thailand, South Africa, and Jordan

I taught classes in Kenya, Singapore, Thailand, and Jordan through the years. Each time I offered these courses I would engage the president in conversations about his knowledge and experiences as he had traveled in these countries. I found it most helpful. After returning from these assignments, I would again discuss my findings with him.

President Patterson was delighted that the International Mission Board, jointly with the North Carolina Baptist State Convention, asked me to present lectures to the Baptist churches across South Africa on the challenges of Islam. He wanted me to give his greetings to the missionaries associated with the Baptist College in Cape Town.

President's Support for Me to Visit Former Soviet Countries

Early in the Patterson presidency I was asked by the IMB along with other professors of missions to travel to the former Soviet Union in designated emerging countries to observe the changing conditions and determine strategies for sending missionaries. My two countries were Kazakhstan and Uzbekistan. Other professors were assigned other countries. We all then met in Tashkent with IMB personnel to discuss our findings.

President's Support for Me to Give a Major Address at a Marathon Meeting at Ridgecrest

Upon my return to campus, I soon traveled to the Baptist Assembly at Ridgecrest along with President Patterson and Dean Bush to attend a 24-hour marathon assembly on Christian Missions to the world of Islam. The gathering was called by the IMB for all heads of all agencies in the SBC and included other guests. It was publicized as an urgent meeting to meet the urgent challenge of global Islam.

There were several hundred select guests including the agency heads of the International Mission Board, North American Mission Board, Christian Life Commission, Lifeway, and the presidents of the six seminaries. There were four major speakers including Dr. Jimmy Draper and myself. President Patterson thought it was a resounding success for meeting a crucial need in global missions.

Three Legs of President Patterson's Vision for Missions in Theological Education

President Patterson saw a significant increase in student enrolment and finances. His vision for theological education and its relation to the churches in preaching and education, in planting new churches in the nation, and in missions to the nations began to unfold.

First, he established a PhD program. His vision was to train future leaders in the churches, universities, and seminaries. My mentoring Dr. Ant Greenham is an example.

Second, he supported the construction of the new building which became the Center for Great Commission Studies. This Center supervised the two-plus-two program which sent hundreds of students into the mission fields. I, personally, taught students in this program who later became pastors of strategic churches, and deans and provosts in seminaries both in the states and abroad, as well as authors of important books of theology and missions.

Third, he established Southeastern College which offered majors in biblical studies and in teaching in the public, charter, and homeschooling areas. Thus, the college was a springboard for students to enter the seminary and to become teachers in the secular elementary and high schools. Many of these students sat in my classes and excelled in their studies.

Surprised to Receive Distinguisged Professorship and Alumni of the Year

I had received the Faculty in Excellence award the last year of President Lolley's tenure. To my utter surprise Dean Russ Bush came to my office to tell me at the board of trustee meeting that they had affirmed the president's recommendation that my faculty title become Distinguished Professor of Missions and World Religions. I told Dean Bush that the change was problematic for me. I continued to tell him when I joined the faculty there were two professors with that title and that I heard sentiments among the faculty of negative expressions. I had not sought such a title and did not need it in any way. Dean Bush replied that it was the president's action and that he himself thought it well deserved.

President Patterson served terms as president of the Southern Baptist Convention. One day I received a call from Vice President Bart Neal that I had been chosen the seminary alumnus of the year. He continued that President Patterson wanted to give me the award at the seminary luncheon during the annual SBC meeting held in Atlanta. I responded that I was appreciative of the award but that I would rather it be given to another. I added that I really had never relished being a convention attendee.

The next day Dr. Neal called and asked if he could visit us at our house. He came and urged us to reconsider receiving the alumnus of the year award. He told us that President Patterson really wanted Joan and me to come to Atlanta to receive the award. He emphasized that there would be no expectation to attend the convention. We could fly down for an overnight stay at the hotel, attend the seminary luncheon, receive the award, and return to Wake Forest. Joan agreed. We received the award which included the gift of a Shofar from President Patterson which I did not blow and returned to Wake Forest.

Behind the Scenes in Tennis Games

Since the very first surprise meeting with Dr. Patterson in my Stealey Hall faculty office when he mentioned playing tennis, tennis became a meeting ground for good exercise and casual conversations. In time there were regular double tennis matches between Patterson and his teammate, Professor Gerald Cowen, and me and my teammate, Professor Josef Solc. As earlier indicated Dr. Solc was an acclaimed tennis player on the national and international stage. Dr. Cowen was a good player. Dr. Patterson and I had athletic ability, but each needed our partners to cover our play. I was athletic in baseball and some golf with my sons. But I needed Dr. Solc to cover for me. Dr. Patterson was a tireless player who never gave up.

I do not recall that Dr. Solc and I ever lost a match. Dr. Patterson chased every ball. Dr. Cowen would throw his racket into the air in disgust. But the matches would continue through the years for several hours a night on the old lighted tennis courts of the old Wake Forest Country Club. We four greatly enjoyed the very good exercise and the times of our informal conversations about world events and happenings in global missions and sometimes in the Southern Baptist Convention.

Dr. Patterson would pick my brain about Iran and global missions. He was interested in my Iranian experience in the writing of my PhD dissertation. I told him my thesis was that, before the Iranian Revolution, the civil religion of the Shah was in conflict with the traditional religion of the Ayatollah. The orthodoxy and fundamental beliefs of the Ayatollah would eventually triumph over the liberalism of the Shah. His ears perked up and the conversation veered to happenings in the Southern Baptist Convention.

Upon his inquiry we discussed the role of women in Iran. I indicated that my last year as a missionary in Iran, the Muslim Dean of the Faculty of Islamic Theology of the University of Teheran placed in my class of Muslim clergy several Iranian women in their veils. This caused great unrest among the clergy. The president asked me how I handled the situation. I told him the women sat in the back of the room upon mandate of the clergy.

Often during water breaks and while Dr. Patterson tended to his dog tied to the fence outside, we would respond to his asking us our opinions on campus matters.

Early in his presidency we talked about the length of faculty meetings. I had suggested that a one-hour limit be placed on meetings, and if the meeting was to proceed beyond the hour, the faculty would have to make a motion. He heartily agreed. I made the motion. It passed.

Conversations about the Emergence of Campbell University Divinity School

On one occasion I had been asked by the president of Campbell University, in Buies Creek south of Raleigh, to serve on a three-person committee to come to campus to conduct a survey of administration, faculty, students, and alumni as to meeting a need for founding a divinity school. Before going to Campbell, I told President Patterson that I would miss the faculty meeting and gave the reason.

Later during a tennis match he wanted to know the result of the Campbell visit. I told him that our committee found an overwhelming interest in the university beginning a divinity school and reported our findings to President Wallace who, by the way, was a Southeastern graduate. He smiled and said that probably more divinity schools and seminaries would follow. He mentioned the Baptist Seminary of Richmond and asked me if my former colleagues there were doing well.

I told him that I was serving as president of the board of directors of the Center for the Christian Understanding of Islam founded by my close friend, Dr. Charles Beckett, a former SBC missionary to Pakistan. Service on the board was completely voluntary. I had negotiated with the president of the Baptist Seminary in Richmond, my former Southeastern colleague, to rent a small office space for Dr. Beckett. We agreed on $300 a month rent which the Board members contributed. Thus, we moved the "Center" from the Beckett dining room table to the seminary. And Dr. Beckett and I would visit mosques throughout the state of Virginia and hold conferences in churches on ministry and missions to Muslims.

President Patterson asked me from time to time how the ministry was going in Richmond. I told him that Dr. Beckett and I and the laypeople on the board were convinced of the need for our ministry. I also mentioned that I was probably away from home too much with this additional completely voluntary ministry by all of us. And I told him that neither Dr. Beckett nor I were ever invited to speak in a seminary class or chapel. His response was that such disinterest was amazing.

The President, the Former Dean, and a Professor

I received a call from former dean Dr. Morris Ashcraft. He and Dr. Lolley left the seminary at the same time. Dr. Ashcraft asked me if I would help support a Habitat for Humanity house in Wake Forest. He asked my opinion about his discussing the idea with President Patterson of the seminary sponsoring a house. I encouraged him to do so.

President Patterson invited Dr. Ashcraft to address the faculty. The result was very positive, and a house was built. I personally gave money as well as labor, as did other members of the seminary family. Dr. Ashcraft had been a fighter pilot in the Korean War. He was a kind spirit and his outreach to President Patterson exemplified a depth of Christian generosity.

President Patterson and Dr. and Mrs. Binkley

Upon retirement the Binkleys moved to a small house across the street from the seminary president's house. When greater health concerns necessitated their move to an assisted living facility in Wake Forest, their financial situation was meager. President Patterson implemented a seminary financial aid plan which supported the Binkleys in their later years.

President Patterson, Chapel, and Braswell

As a faculty member I made a commitment to be present in chapel services held weekly. The president had expectations that faculty should be present in chapel services for worship as well as setting examples for the students. President Patterson especially expected faculty to attend chapel.

President Patterson invited the "big guns," in strategic churches and in the SBC agencies, to speak in chapel. Often during our tennis matches he would tell us ahead of time about upcoming speakers. Sometimes in their introductory remarks they would express their joy of the new days at Southeastern under Patterson's leadership. I once told President Patterson that I went to chapel for worship and not to hear negative remarks about the past. He told me that he spoke with the speakers in his office each time before chapel and encouraged them to be positive.

I always heard President Patterson's messages in chapel. They were instructional and inspirational. I felt like it was a true worship service.

Fallout from the Release of a Student Letter from Amman

One of the most crucial relationships I had with President Patterson resulted from my teaching assignment with the two-plus-two students meeting in Amman, Jordan. Some thirty students gathered, some single and some with families, from various countries including Somalia, Lebanon, and Iraq. Their mission was to Muslim peoples, and my class was about missions to Muslims.

Before I concluded the class to head back to Wake Forest, the students asked me if they could send a letter they had drafted with me to be released to the *Baptist Press* and other Baptist publications. The letter basically asked Southern Baptists to be sensitive in their comments about the Muslim prophet Muhammad and about Muslims generally. The students indicated that in the countries where they were missionaries one needed to be sensitive about castigating Islam. They were there to share the gospel.

I read the letter and found it a very sensitive and responsible request. I asked the students if they supported the letter one hundred percent. They replied yes. I asked the students if they saw in the letter any negative view of the International Mission Board. They replied no. And thirdly I asked the class if they thought the release of the letter would bring any negative views toward Southeastern Seminary. They replied no. All students affirmed sending the letter.

I arrived back in Wake Forest on the weekend. On Monday, from my office, I released the letter to *Baptist Press* and to Baptist publications in several states. The result was calls to my office from the *New York Times*, *Boston Globe*, and *Baptist Press* for further comments on the contents of the letter. I always replied that the students were sharing the gospel in the trenches in difficult circumstances. They were not there to debate issues on a public stage.

The background which instigated the concerns of the students were comments made by a Southern Baptist Convention leader and high-profile Baptist minister which were carried in world presses that the founder of the religion of Islam was a pedophile. The minister's comments were inspired by a university professor's book on Islam. The minister was a close friend of President Patterson, and the professor was mentored by Patterson in his PhD studies.

In the meantime, President and Mrs. Patterson stopped in Amman, Jordan, as their last stop in visiting seminary students in other countries. Patterson learned of the letter and called Dean Bush Monday evening to tell me not to release the letter. It was too late.

Afterward he called Dean Bush again for him to tell me to meet him in his office upon his return.

I never went to the president's office. He never mentioned it to me again. Having been a missionary to a 98% Muslim population, I knew the sensitivities one needed to have to share the gospel. One was not to castigate the founder of their religion. The students had shared in class the extreme challenges they faced to have entre with Muslim peoples.

Their country presses had carried the comments of the high-profile SBC leader. Those comments did not help them in their challenging mission to share the gospel in the trenches with Muslim peoples.

Braswells and Personal Relationships with the Pattersons

Joan and I will never forget the personal outreach to us by President and Mrs. Patterson.

Our daughter returned to Wake Forest from her work at the United States embassy in Damascus, Syria, to give birth to our first grandchild, Dana Alexandra Jordan, at Rex

Hospital in Raleigh. Infant Dana in her baby carriage was rolled from our North Main Street home to the seminary campus. We paused at the gazebo and out walks President Patterson to greet her and welcome her to Southeastern Seminary. He said when she was old enough that he would serve her ice cream in his office. As she grew older, Dana visited us grandparents in the summertime when her parents were on home leave from their various assignments in embassies in Damascus, Amman, Tunis, and Paris. Dana would bike with me around the campus and meet at the gazebo. And sure enough President Patterson provided her that promised ice cream.

Our youngest daughter who had been born in Teheran, Iran, wanted to have her wedding ceremony at the campus gazebo and wanted me to officiate. President and Mrs. Patterson initiated the offer to provide chairs for the outdoor ceremony and floral arrangements.

Mrs. Patterson also spoke with Joan and offered rooms in the campus guest house for our out-of-town guests.

The most tragic happening in our life as a family was the discovery of cancer in Dana's leg when her family was about to leave for their assignment at the embassy in Rabat, Morocco.

They stayed in Washington, D.C. for two years while Dana received treatment at the Children's Hospital at Georgetown University. She fought the disease with bravery reading her French books, in which she was fluent, and utilizing her artwork. She died at fourteen years of age in the hospital. It crushed my heart. And it has weighed on my heart ever since. I immediately established the Dana Alexander Jordan Scholarship at Wake Forest Baptist Church which would be granted a deserving high school graduate each year.

At that time, Dr. Patterson had moved from Southeastern Seminary to be president of Southwestern Seminary. And I had retired from Southeastern and joined the faculty of Campbell University Divinity School as Senior Professor of World Religions and founding director of the World Religion and Global Cultures Center. Unbeknown to Joan and me someone informed him of Dana's death. We received letters from both the Pattersons and later a note from the church about their gift to the scholarship.

The last time I saw the Pattersons was in the seminary cemetery at the burial of Dean Russ Bush. We greeted each other with hugs.

President and Professor Shared Vision and Programs in Excellence in Theological Education

The Braswells shall never forget the personal and unsolicited kindnesses of Paige and Dorothy Patterson to the Braswell family. He was a good president and friend to me both in our working together to foster excellence in the classroom and lovingkindness in the global missionary outreach. Just perhaps the game of tennis first mentioned in my office before Dr. Patterson was elected president throughout our playing days provided the fuel for our professional and our personal friendship.

10

INTERIM PRESIDENT BART C. NEAL

2003-2004

A BRIEF HISTORY

Upon Dr. Patterson's move to serve as president of Southwestern Baptist Theological Seminary, Dr. Bart Neal served as interim president of Southeastern Baptist Theological Seminary beginning in July 2003. He filled the role of president starting July 21 and would serve until Dr. Daniel Akin's election as president the following year.

Bart Neal was born in Conroe, Texas, and attended Baylor University where he earned his Bachelor of Music degree in 1968, as well as his Master of Religious Education from New Orleans Baptist Theological Seminary the same year. He was ordained in 1966 and served as a minister of music at churches in Texas, Louisiana, Georgia, and Arkansas. He married Edith Latta Neal who was also from Texas and also earned her degree in music. They had two children, and both possessing backgrounds in music, Dr. and

Mrs. Neal would often perform together at various conferences and programs.[1]

In 1981 Dr. Neal completed his Doctor of Education at New Orleans Baptist Theological Seminary. He also worked at that seminary from 1978 until 1993 and served in several capacities including Director of Admissions and Registrar, Vice President for Development, and Assistant Professor of Church Administration.[2]

He came to Southeastern from New Orleans in the summer of 1993 and served as Vice President for Institutional Advancement. During his time at Southeastern, Dr. Neal helped lead the "Scholarship on Fire!" fundraising effort which continued into Dr. Akin's presidency. He was also Professor of Christian Education.[3]

Upon Dr. Patterson's resignation, Dr. Neal led Southeastern as interim president from July 2003 until January 2004. He returned to his position as Vice President for Institutional Advancement after Dr. Akin was elected president. In the fall of 2005, Dr. Neal retired after serving Southeastern for over ten years.[4]

BRASWELL AND NEAL

Experience with President

Dr. Bart Neal was an excellent colleague. President Patterson selected him for Vice President for Institutional Advancement and a professorship in Christian Education. They were students together at New Orleans Baptist Theological Seminary and friends afterward.

The Board of Trustees appointed Dr. Neal Interim President in July 2003 after President Patterson assumed the presidency of Southwestern Baptist Theological Seminary. He served in the office six months before Dr. Daniel Akin was elected president in January 2004.

As a faculty colleague Dr. Neal was always kind and considerate in his relations with me. I have already mentioned the episode with a Doctor of Ministry student in which we together held fast to academic standards with the backing of President Patterson.

When my mother died, Dr. Neal with his assistant, Marty Jacumin, attended the funeral service in Emporia, Virginia. It was a two-hundred-mile round trip, so their attendance surprised me. They gave up quality time. I was surprised to see them in the service. I have never forgotten their kindness.

I have mentioned the time when Dr. Neal visited our home on North Main Street to urge us on behalf of President Patterson to travel to Atlanta during the SBC meeting to attend the seminary luncheon to receive the alumni of the year award. His "pastoral" and winsome visit persuaded us to go.

Perhaps the most memorable thing to happen with my relationship with Interim President Neal demonstrates his character and approach to colleagues.

I was thinking of retiring about the time of this seminary administrative change. Campbell University Divinity School leadership several years prior had asked me to join their faculty. At the time of Interim President Neal, I had served on the faculty some thirty years. I had even outlasted President Patterson.

I had maintained two offices at the insistence of President Patterson. My office on the third floor of Stealey Hall had too many loaded filing cabinets and bookshelves compared to my neat and orderly office in Jacumin-Simpson.

So, I contacted the office of the Director of Plant Services to leave a message that I would appreciate any assistance to move books and boxes of papers to my truck parked in a Stealey Hall parking space so I could take them to my house. The director called me to tell me that it was not the responsibility of his department to assist.

Somehow word got out from the department to Interim President Neal. When I was at lunch at home Interim President Neal called and asked if he might come for a brief visit. He came quickly with his assistant and, over tea and cookies which Joan assembled, he profusely apologized for the refusal of the director to assist me. He said that for anything I needed moved to my house there would be help with a seminary truck and workers. And he added again an apology.

That was Interim President Bart Neal. I believe he would have done it for any faculty member. To me he was a colleague and a friend and a good interim president. I shall always remember his pastoral relations to my family and to the seminary family.

11

PRESIDENT DANIEL L. AKIN

2004-PRESENT

A BRIEF HISTORY

Following the presidency of Dr. Patterson and the interim of Dr. Neal, Dr. Daniel Akin was selected as the next president of Southeastern Baptist Theological Seminary. He would serve longer than any previous president of the seminary and bring with him a heart for missions and theological education.

Dr. Akin was born January 1957 in Atlanta, Georgia. Initially interested in pursuing a career in sports, he focused his attention on baseball when he attended college. While a promising athlete, a series of events interrupted his original plans and directed him toward fulltime ministry. During a mission trip in 1977 he clearly felt this call into ministry. In the months leading up to this, he had participated in local ministry with his church which stirred his heart for reaching his neighbors.[1] Reflecting on these experiences, Dr. Akin expressed he had grown to understand that "My neighbor may live across the street, but he or she may also live across the nation or in a different part of the world. If they need to be loved and cared for in Jesus' name, no matter *who* they are or *where* they live, they are my neighbors."[2] This firmly rooted love for neighbor and the nations would play a crucial role in the future of Southeastern Seminary.

After this Dr. Akin started classes at Criswell College and pursued a Bachelor of Arts in Biblical Studies, graduating in 1980. He then finished his Master of Divinity at Southwestern Baptist Theological Seminary in 1983, followed by his Doctor of Philosophy at the University of Texas at Arlington in 1989. He had married Charlotte Bourne on May 27, 1978, and together they raised four sons, all of whom would enter fields of ministry.[3]

Teaching and pastoring characterized Dr. Akin's career. He served numerous churches and as early as 1988 began teaching at Criswell College as professor of New Testament, Theology, and Church History. Here he also took on the leadership role as the Dean of Students. In 1992 he moved to Southeastern Baptist Theological Seminary to serve as Dean of Students and an Associate Professor of Theology.[4] In these roles he sought to help students develop strong theology, cultivate a life honoring God, and build skills in expository preaching.[5]

In 1996, Dr. Akin moved to Kentucky and became the Dean of the School of Theology and Senior Vice President for Academic Administration at Southern Baptist Theological Seminary until 2004. He also served as a professor for theology and preaching during these years.[6]

Then, in January 2004, he was hired as president of Southeastern Baptist Theological Seminary and would again serve as Professor of Preaching and Theology. His inauguration took place on October 27, 2004.[7] A heart for the Great Commission would characterize Dr. Akin's presidency. He pursued a seminary program which would "wed the head, the heart, and the hands in fulfilling the Great Commission of the Lord Jesus Christ."[8] His presidency saw an increased and intertwined focus on missions, theological training, and partnerships to deepen education and increase the reach of theological training.

President Akin took the foundation laid since the seminary's earliest years, the vision cast by Dr. Drummond, and the infrastructure begun by Dr. Patterson, and propelled forward the centrality of the Great Commission to every facet of Southeastern. In 2006 a new mission statement and motto were embraced by the seminary. The mission statement "Southeastern Baptist Theological Seminary seeks to glorify the Lord Jesus Christ by equipping students to serve the Church and fulfill the Great Commission" (Matt. 28:19-20) and the motto "Every classroom a Great Commission classroom" truly represented Dr. Akin's desire to see all students in all ministries be trained to reach the world.[9]

The seminary developed significantly under these guiding statements. Numerous degrees, partnerships, and initiatives began during these years. In addition to missions, Dr. Akin also focused on expository preaching at the seminary. Along with being a Great Commission seminary, Dr. Akin said, "it would be equally correct to say of our school that, 'Southeastern Baptist Theological Seminary is an Expository Preaching Seminary.'"[10] Under his influence, the seminary continued to train students in expositional methods and emphasize programs in expository preaching.

The seminary also broadened access to theological education during Dr. Akin's presidency. The seminary continued to offer certificate courses to help train those who could not attend school full-time or wanted additional theological training. Distance learning opportunities continued and 2013 saw the development of Southeastern's first Master of Divinity program to be offered entirely online.[11] Dr. Akin also oversaw the creation of the North Carolina Field Minister Program. This program allows long-term inmates to receive education while in prison through the College at Southeastern.[12]

Though many of these were new initiatives, this desire to train laypeople, and those outside the immediate radius of the seminary, existed from the very start of Southeastern.

Since Southeastern's earliest years, partnerships with organizations and churches played vital roles in the training of students. The significance of these partnerships and a desire to increase the reach of that invaluable training led to the development of a program known as the Global Theological Initiatives (GTI). GTI seeks to employ the resources of SEBTS to benefit theological education through strategic partnerships around the world. GTI also developed the Hispanic, Persian, and East Asian Leadership initiatives, which provide courses and training in the native languages of people in these regions, thereby increasing the worldwide reach of theological training.[13]

Dr. Akin's heart for missions has been evident through the trajectory of the seminary, its partnerships, and his own involvement in mission work. Partnerships with organizations such as the IMB and NAMB continue. The seminary also informs students of missions by spotlighting missionaries, people groups, and areas of the world to pray for in chapel each week. These partnerships and practices have shaped the vision of the seminary and help its staff and its students to cultivate a heart for missions in all areas of ministry.

Dr. Akin's writing emphasizes the relationship between theological education and the Great Commission. He is series editor and author in the *Christ-Centered Exposition Commentary* series, has authored further books focused on theology, and has penned several books on missions. He coauthored *Pastoral Theology* and wrote *10 Who Changed the World* which draws on the stories of ten missionaries from history. His heart for families is also clear through his book *Raising Kids with a Heart for Mission*.[14]

Dr. Akin's presidency brought further growth to historically central desires of Southeastern's presidents. Dr. Stealey's tripod of education at Southeastern to train pastors, missionaries, and educators for ministry has been carried on by each successive president with their particular strengths. The strands of evangelism and theological education are threaded throughout the various practical and academic initiatives of the school. In similar fashion, Dr. Akin captured this same heart by infusing into each facet of education and ministry at Southeastern the central call of the Great Commission so that all students are sent out with thorough education and sights set on the mission of all Christian ministry.

BRASWELL AND AKIN

Experience with President

Dr. Danny Akin as a Faculty Colleague

President Patterson brought Dr. Akin to join the seminary faculty from Criswell College. Dr. Akin assumed the positions of Associate Professor of Theology and Dean of Students. I remember that students flocked to his systematic theology classes and would tell me of the helpful outlines he provided. He accepted the mentoring of Doctor of Ministry students cheerfully and we worked together on committees. When he left to join the Southern Seminary faculty in 1996, he willingly concluded his supervision of a DMin student when he could easily have requested that another faculty member take his place.

He was an excellent colleague, and I regretted to see him leave with his devoted relationship to his classes and to the wellbeing of the seminary community. There was one thing President Patterson and I could not persuade him to do. We would ask him to join us in tennis doubles. He was much wiser than we.

My Retirement under President Akin

I had planned to retire in December after serving on the faculty for over thirty years as Dr. Akin was assuming the office of president in January 2004. Campbell University Divinity School, since its founding in 1996, had urged me to join their faculty. I did join its faculty in January 2005 as senior professor after retiring December 31, 2004. The seminary faculty provided a retirement luncheon and unveiled the traditional portrait.

Dean Bush delivered generous remarks, and President Akin voiced his kind words.

Invitation to Teach at Southeastern while on the Faculty at Campbell University Divinity School

In 2006 I became the founding director of the World Religion and Global Cultures Center of Campbell Divinity School which upon my second retirement was named the George W. Braswell and Margaret Joan Braswell World Religions and Global Cultures Center in 2016. The Center was a dream come true for me.

I had been offered a professorship at Baylor University twice during the Drummond presidency to join its faculty and build a center for Islamic studies. Both times Joan and I felt led to remain at Southeastern.

While at Campbell University Divinity School Dean Russ Bush, with the blessings of President Akin, asked me to be Fletcher Visiting Professor of Missions in 2006, 2007, and

2010 to offer my old course I had founded at Southeastern in 1982. I was happy that President Akin and Dean Bush gave me this opportunity to be a part of the seminary community that Joan and I had joined in 1974 as we returned from Iran.

President Akin's Generosity and Vision for Placement of the Water Fountain at the Gazebo in Memory of Our Granddaughter

I discussed with President Akin in 2015 an idea that I had nourished for some time.

Our granddaughter Dana had died of cancer at age fourteen in 2007. During her summertime visits with Joan and me we would ride bikes playing hide and seek around the campus. I asked President Akin if we might plant a tree or small flower garden on campus in her memory.

He arranged to take Joan and me and Executive Vice President Hutchinson to lunch for further discussion. Utterly to our surprise he suggested a water fountain inside the Gazebo and that the seminary would purchase it and maintain it. We joyfully said we would like to purchase the fountain with a French motif design since Dana was fluent in French. He replied that the seminary would then install and maintain it.

He and Mr. Hutchinson also installed a plaque with notation and included the quote from the book of Revelation (7:17): "For the Lamb which is in the midst of the throne shall feed them, and shall lead them unto living fountains of water: and God shall wipe away all tears from their eyes."

Dr. Akin's decision to place the water fountain inside the gazebo has attracted untold families with their children to gather around the foundation to listen to the waterfall and to touch the water flow. Untold numbers of students have found it a place for study and prayer as they sit around it and hear the gentle water flow. And all walking traffic from Stealey Hall to Binkley Chapel walk around it.

I would never have thought of the memorial water fountain. President Akin was a great visionary that has affected the lives of so many students and townspeople and other visitors to the campus who pause at the fountain for refreshment.

President Akin's Vision and Programs for Global Missions

President Akin has written that once he began to travel to countries where two-plus-two students were assigned to be missionaries with the IMB, he was greatly inspired to prepare all seminary emphases around global missions, both home and international.

The Persian Leadership Initiative

Soon he assisted in bringing to the campus an Iranian man, Kambiz, who grew up as a Muslim in Iran. He harassed Christians. He was miraculously converted to faith in Jesus Christ, and then became a student at Southeastern. He became director of the program named the Persian Leadership Initiative.

The Persian Leadership Initiative has developed cours-es in Farsi and over the internet is reaching thousands of Farsi-speakers around the globe with Bible and theology courses. It is a unique program not offered elsewhere.

As Joan and I were the first appointed missionaries to Iran by the IMB in 1967, we rejoice in this special and need-ed Persian Leadership Initiative. We established the Braswell Persian Initiative Endowment with the blessing of President Akin and his staff.

Out of the blue, one of my former doctoral students, Dr. Vince Hefner, who is pastor of a missionary-minded and giving church, learned of the endowment, called me, and after holding a church conference offered a very gener-ous gift to the endowment. President Akin invited him, his wife Sherry, Joan, me, and other staff to a luncheon in ap-preciation for the gift. President Akin was linking missions to an Iran of the past to present Iran with the establishment of the Persian Initiative. No other seminary or religious en-tity is involved in such a ministry.

Inspiration to Me from President Akin's Book, *10 Who Changed the World*

Mike Dishman, a deacon, and I at Wake Forest Baptist Church conducted a research project to determine the num-ber of missionaries appointed by SBC mission agencies who had at some time in their lives been members of Wake Forest Baptist Church. We found that there were some one hundred and forty beginning with Matthew and Eliza Yates in 1848.

We initiated a plan to build a wall display. I provided the finances to build an eight-foot rounded globe. Mike placed flags on the globe in each country where missionaries had served. Plaques were wall-mounted with their names and countries of missionary service. And the bold inscription BEYOND THE WALLS was placed above the globe.

I used President Akin's book *10 Who Changed the World* for a Wednesday night study leading up to the dedication of the BEYOND THE WALLS display in the foyer of the educational building. On the Wednesday evening for the dedication President and Mrs. Akin attended. I was honored by their presence around the supper table and their support for BEYOND THE WALLS.

President Akin's Support of the George Braswell Missions and World Religions Library Located in the Center for Great Commission Studies

One day I was approached by Southeastern mission faculty and library staff to consider giving my library to the seminary to be placed in the Sam James Conference Room in the Center for Great Commission Studies. I had not thought of that possibility.

Sam James was a student with Joan and me at Wake Forest College on this campus. Sam and Rachel were missionaries to Vietnam, and I invited him to lead a revival when I was pastor of Cullowhee Baptist Church at Western Carolina University and they were on home leave. When we and our families later were both on home leave from

Vietnam and Iran, Sam and I studied and graduated with the first Doctor of Ministry class at Southeastern.

After I joined the seminary faculty, Sam was director of the IMB missionary center in Richmond and invited me for several years to give lectures there. And to cap it off when Sam was director for missionaries in Asia, he asked me to conduct a church growth survey across the island of Taiwan involving missionaries and nationals.

Responding to their request I said that since it is the Sam James Conference Room why not put his books and Vietnam items in it. They said that President Akin blessed this request for my library to be included. Thus, in September 2019 the George Braswell Missions and World Religions Library was dedicated with President Akin's speech, with a host of guests, and with a delicious luncheon.

Again, the vision and spirit of global missions is at the heart of President Akin's missionary vision and action. Classes, seminars, and trustee committee meetings are held in the Sam James Conference Room and George Braswell Missions and World Religions Library. One cannot but help wonder about global missions in such a setting. Who would have thought of the James and the Braswell families together again on this very campus since beginning their friendship here in 1954?

President Akin's Support of Three Writing Projects

In the last three years, President Akin has affirmed three research and writing projects involving me.

Fourteen Journeys

I was provided an office with a computer in Stephens-Mackie Hall and a research assistant named Brian Min. The outcome was a manuscript *Fourteen Journeys*. I gave the copyright to the seminary with all royalties to go to the Braswell Persian Initiative Endowment. The seminary's office of marketing and communications designed the cover, published the manuscript via Amazon, and publicized the book in various media.

Practicum in World Religions

Second, Provost Whitfield assigned Colleen Hall, a research assistant, to assist me in the research and writing project to evaluate the impact of a course I inaugurated as a faculty member in 1982 named Practicum in World Religions. The class emerged from a grant I received from ATS to study the status and impact of world religion communities upon Christianity and churches and theological education. The class has continued in the seminary curriculum. Several thousand students and church members have been impacted by the class.

Colleen and I created questionnaires and mailed them to former students and church folk who had participated in the class. We also interviewed in hour sessions eight former students as to their views on the value of the class when they were a part of it and how it had influenced their ministries and churches since their class experience. The results of the study became a published paper.

Seven Presidents and One Professor

Third, Provost Whitfield, with President Akin's approval, assigned to me Rachel Alley, a research assistant, to assist in the research and writing of the present title *Seven Presidents and One Professor*. This writing is composed of my own experiences of knowing all seven presidents of Southeastern Baptist Seminary and serving with six of them.

Appreciation to President Akin

As a retired Distinguished Professor Emeritus of Missions and World Religions I am most grateful to President Akin for his every kindness to Joan and me, for his deep commitment to global missions, and for his providing time and space for an 86-year-old to recall cherished memories of Iran and seminary classrooms and colleagueship with faculty and with knowing and serving with the seven presidents of Southeastern Baptist Theological Seminary.

12

CONCLUSION

I have been most fortunate to have Joan and the four children to affirm and enjoy living in Wake Forest, attending its schools and Wake Forest Baptist Church, and being a part of the seminary campus and family.

My memories of the seven seminary presidents began in high school with President Stealey coming to my home church to speak. They continue with President Binkley providing opportunities for my family to live in a missionary house, for me to teach a course as a visiting professor while on home leave as a missionary in Iran, and later for the invitation to join the faculty.

Then I served with President Lolley for fourteen years, with President Drummond for four years, with President Patterson for eleven years, with Interim President Neal for 6 months, and served with President Akin as faculty colleagues and for a year before my retirement. Afterward I served as a visiting professor and then as a colleague until the present.

The presidents in so many ways have related to me in friendship, in colleagueship, and in providing opportunities and encouragement to be the best classroom teacher I could be.

They supported my research, writing, and publication of articles and books. The presidents also affirmed my interim pastorates and ministries in the churches, as well as my many assignments with the home and foreign mission boards of the SBC.

By the vision and hard work of these presidents God has provided the Braswell family blessed opportunities of ministry and mission. Other professors would have their own personal stories to tell. In these latter days it does appear that I am the only professor left with the knowledge and experience of serving with the seven presidents. Thus I believe that they have followed the path given them by the Lord Jesus Christ and have impacted thousands of men, women, and families in the life of Southeastern Baptist Theological Seminary. I trust that I along with them have experienced the same. To God be the Glory.

INFLUENCES OF FAMILY, FAITH, CHURCH, FRIENDS, COLLEAGUES, AND NEIGHBORS OVER A LIFETIME

PERSONAL AND FAMILY HISTORY

Born May 30, 1936 in Emporia, Virginia, to George W. and Lillie P. Braswell

Graduated Greenville County High School, 1954.

Ordained by Main Street Baptist Church, Emporia, Virginia, 1962

Married **Margaret Joan Owen**, June 14, 1958, Born December 26, 1935; daughter of Drs. R. H. and M. L. Owen of Canton, North Carolina; BS Wake Forest University, 1958; teacher; further Studies at Western Carolina University and Southeastern Baptist Theological Seminary

Children

Margaret Anne Jordan (BA Wake Forest University; MA in Arabic Studies from Georgetown University; MA in French Literature from Middlebury College program in Paris, France; PhD in French Language and Literature from the University of Maryland; formerly with U.S. Embassy in Damascus, Amman, Tunis, Paris, Algiers, and Mauritania; retired in Wake Forest to Samuel Wait House built 1843.)

George Robert (BS UNC Chapel Hill; MA Clinical Psychology at Western Carolina University; formerly employed as psychologist with Dorothea Dix Hospital, Northeastern North Carolina school systems; and presently independent psychologist in Wake Forest.)

William Brien (BS Guilford College; employed as Teacher-Coach at Jamestown-Ragsdale High School, Jamestown, North Carolina), coached seven state soccer championships, inducted into North Carolina Soccer Hall of Fame and the Guilford County Hall of Fame.

Rebecca Joy Edwards (BA Wake Forest University; MSW University of Southern Indiana), formerly employed with school system in Evansville, Indiana, presently owner of Mind Over Matters counseling services in Newburgh, Indiana and in St. Louis, Missouri.

Grandchildren

Dana Alexandra Jordan (1992–2007)
Milan Owen Edwards (b. 1999, Evansville, Indiana)
Margaret Isabel Edwards (b. 2001, Evansville, Indiana)
Emerson Mae Edwards (b. 2009, Evansville, Indiana)

EDUCATION

BA in Philosophy and History, Wake Forest University, 1958

BD (Master of Divinity) in Missions, Yale University Divinity School, 1961

MA in Cultural Anthropology University of North Carolina at Chapel Hill, 1973

DMin in Theology/Missions, Southeastern Baptist Theological Seminary, 1973

PhD in Cultural Anthropology, University of North Carolina at Chapel Hill, 1975

EXPERIENCE

2005–Present	Senior Professor of World Religions, Campbell Divinity School
2007–2016	Retired Founding Director, World Religions and Global Cultures Center, Campbell University Divinity School

Seven Presidents and One Professor

1997–2008	President (Voluntary Service), Beckett Center for Christian Understanding of Islam
2006, 2007, 2010	Fletcher Visiting Professor of Missions, Southeastern Baptist Seminary
2004–present	Distinguished Professor of Missions and World Religions Emeritus, Southeastern Baptist Theological Seminary
1998–2004	Distinguished Professor of Missions and World Religions, Southeastern Baptist Theological Seminary
1991–2002	Director, Doctor of Ministry Program, Southeastern Baptist Theological Seminary
1978–1998	Professor of Missions and World Religions, Southeastern Baptist Theological Seminary
1974–1978	Associate Professor of Church History and Missions, Southeastern Baptist Theological Seminary
1973–1974	Professor of History, Damavand College, Tehran, Iran
1972–1973	Visiting Teacher in Missions, Southeastern Baptist Theological Seminary
1968–1974	Professor of English and Comparative Religions, Faculty of Islamic Theology of the University of Tehran, Iran

1968–1972	Associate Director, Armaghan Institute, Tehran, Iran
1967–1974	Missionary of Foreign Mission Board, Southern Baptist Convention, Iran
1962–1967	Minister, Cullowhee Baptist Church, Cullowhee, North Carolina

MEMBERSHIP IN SOCIETIES, HONORS, AND AWARDS

Elected to Phi Beta Kappa Honor Society

Elected to Omicron Delta Kappa Leadership

Society Fellow of American Anthropological Association

Member of American Society of Missiology

Member of The Middle East Studies Association of North America

Association of Theological Schools Competitive Research Grant Recipient, 1980–1981

Recognition Award, Department of Interfaith Witness of Home Mission Board of Southern Baptist Convention, 1986

Faculty Excellence in Teaching Award, Southeastern Baptist Theological Seminary, 1987

Distinguished Professorship by Board of Trustees, Southeastern Baptist Theological Seminary, 1998

Distinguished National Alumnus of the Year, Southeastern Baptist Theological Seminary, 1999

Presidential Award, Southeastern Baptist Theological Seminary, 2002

Recognition by Southeastern Baptist Theological Seminary for thirty years of service, 2003

Professor Emeritus granted by Board of Trustees, Southeastern Baptist Theological Seminary, 2004

Fletcher Visiting Professor of Missions, Southeastern Baptist Theological Seminary, 2006, 2007, 2010

Awarded Honorary Doctor of Divinity, Campbell University, 2006

Faculty Excellence in Teaching Award, Campbell Divinity School, 2008

First Community Award by the Church of Jesus Christ of Latter-day Saints, 2011

Literary Notables of the Wake Forest Birthplace Society and Museum

Honored by naming George W. and Joan O. Braswell World Religions and Global Cultures Center of Campbell University Divinity School, 2016

Honored by establishment of the George and Joan Braswell Iran Room at the Beckett Center in Richmond, VA, 2016

Honored by the establishment and dedication of The George Braswell Missions and World Religions Library located in the Center for Great Commission Studies of Southeastern Baptist Theological Seminary, 2019

Dedication of the George Braswell Mission Room in Honor of the Braswell Bible Study Group at Main Street Baptist Church, Emporia, Virginia on September 18, 2022

Leadership in Church and Community

Leadership in Baptist and Ecumenical Church and Youth Meetings in Beirut, Lebanon; Amman, Jordan; Tel Aviv, Israel; Cairo, Egypt; Tehran, Iran, 1968–1974

Organized Strategy Conference for Baptist Missionaries in ten countries in the Middle East and North Africa held in Tehran, Iran, 1969

Assignment with Foreign Mission Board of the Southern Baptist Convention to Iran, 1967–1974

Special Assignments in summer 1973 and summer 1978

Assignment with Foreign Mission Board (SBC) to Central America (Guatemala, Honduras, Costa Rica), 1977

Assignment with Foreign Mission Board (SBC) to the Middle East (Lebanon, Jordan, Israel, Gaza, Iran), 1978

Assignment with Foreign Mission Board (SBC) to Europe and North Africa (Belgium, France, West Berlin, Switzerland, Morocco), 1980

Assignment with Foreign Mission Board (SBC) to Taiwan, 1987

Assignment with Foreign Mission Board (SBC) to Central Asia, Russia, Kazakhstan, Uzbekistan, 1994

Assignment with Foreign Mission Board (FMB) and North Carolina Baptist State Convention Partnership with South Africa to South Africa (Pretoria, Johannesburg, Durban, and Cape Town) May–June 1997

Sabbatical Consultant to Department of Interfaith Witness of the Home Mission Board (SBC) on Baptist-Muslim Relations, 1980–1981

SEBTS Teaching Assignment to Nairobi, Kenya, January 1997 SEBTS Teaching Assignment to Singapore, January 1999

SEBTS Teaching Assignment to Chiang Mai, Thailand, January 2000, 2001, 2002 SEBTS Teaching Assignment to Manila, Philippines, February 2000, 2001, 2002

SEBTS Teaching Assignment to Amman, Jordan, 2003

Lecturer to Caribbean Baptist Fellowship meeting in Barbados, West Indies, 1997

Research Visits to Israel in 1985; to Damascus, Syria, in 1985; to Damascus, Syria, and Istanbul, Turkey in 1991; to Amman, Jordan, and Israel in 1995

Seminary practica in church planting in cooperation with the Home Mission Board (SBC) in major cities of US and Canada, including Seattle, Portland, San Francisco, Detroit, Chicago, Milwaukee, New York, Boston, Washington, Atlanta, Miami, Baltimore, Philadelphia, Oklahoma City, Charlotte, Raleigh, Greenville, Norfolk, Richmond, Omaha, Toronto, Columbia, Las Vegas, Cincinnati, Buffalo, 1975– 1998

Practicum in world religions held multiple times yearly in settings in Washington, D.C.; Atlanta; New York City; Research Triangle of NC, 1980–2016

Service as Interim Pastor in ten churches; service on Committees of Wake Forest Baptist Church, including chair of diaconate and chair of stewardship committee; co-chair of Beyond the Walls Campaign

Lecturer on Army and Air Force bases in Virginia, North Carolina, South Carolina, Florida, Oklahoma, and Wisconsin on cross-cultural communication, Islam, and the Middle East

Lecturer on multiple university and seminary campuses and in pastors' schools Service on Poteat Scholarship Committee, Wake Forest University, 1991–1995, chair 1993–1995

Founder's Day Address given at Wake Forest University, 1980

Lecturer sponsored by National Endowment for the Humanities at Rice University

EDUCATIONAL ASSIGNMENTS

Southeastern Baptist Theological Seminary Committees including Self Study, Academic Council, Long Range Planning, Graduate Studies, Library, Chapel, Convocation and Special Lectures, Doctor of Ministry (Director and Chair)

Service on Accrediting Committees of Southern Association of Colleges and Universities and the American Theological Schools

PUBLICATIONS AND WRITINGS

Theses

"The Ulama In Four Socio-Cultural Contexts." MA thesis, The University of North Carolina at Chapel Hill, l973.

"Ministry Among Internationals in the Research Triangle Area." DMin report, Southeastern Baptist Theological Seminary, 1973.

"A Mosaic of Mullahs and Mosques: Religion and Politics in Iranian Shiah, Islam." PhD diss., The University of North Carolina at Chapel Hill, 1975.

Books

To Ride A Magic Carpet. Nashville, TN: Broadman, 1977.

Understanding World Religions. Nashville, TN: Broadman, 1983. Korean edition published by Jordan Press in 1986.

Understanding Sectarian Groups in America. Nashville, TN: Broadman, 1986.

Understanding World Religions. Rev. ed. Nashville, TN: Broadman, 1994.

Understanding Sectarian Groups in America. Rev. ed. Nashville, TN: Broadman, 1994

Study Guide on World Religions with Seminary Extension. Nashville: Convention Press, 1994.

Islam: Its Prophet, Peoples, Politics, and Power. Nashville, TN: Broadman & Holman, 1996.

What You Need To Know About Islam and Muslims. Nashville, TN: Broadman & Holman, 2000.

Gura Holman De Religiones Del Mundo: Con Capitulos Especiales Sobre el Islam y el Christianismo. Nashville, TN: Broadman & Holman, 2005.

Islam and America: Answers to the 31 Most Asked Questions. Nashville, TN: Broadman & Holman, 2005.

Crossroads of Religion and Revolution: A Personal Look at Events and Changes Through a Lifetime Journey Among Iranian Muslims and Southern Baptists and Global Religions With Family and Friends. Maitland, FL: Xulon Press, 2012.

From Iran To America: Encounters with Many Faiths. Maitland, FL: Xulon Press, 2014.

14 Journeys: Engaging an Increasingly Pluralistic World With Christian Civility and Charity, Wake Forest, NC: Southeastern Baptist Theological Seminary, 2021.

Articles

"Civil Religion in Contemporary Iran." *Journal of Church and State* 21 (1979): 223–46.

"A Life History of An Iranian Young Man and Modernizing Influences." *Missiology* 7 (1979): 195–209.

"The Shape of Things to Come: Societal and Psychological Dimensions of World Missions." *Perspectives in Religious Studies* 3 (1979): 208–23. Reprinted in *Educating for Christian Missions: Supporting Christian Missions through Education*, ed. Arthur L. Walker, Jr. Nashville, TN: Broadman, 1981.

"Iran and Islam." *Theology Today* 36 (1980): 523–33. Reprinted in *Military Chaplains' Review* (1980).

"Iran: Dreams and Nightmares." *The Christian Century* 97 (July 16–23, 1980): 729.

"The Encounter of Christianity and Islam: The Missionary Theology of Kenneth Cragg." *Perspectives in Religious Studies* 8 (1981): 117–27.

"Communicating Across Barriers." *Faith and Mission* 2 (1985): 35–41.

"Field-Based Learning in World Religions." *Missiology* 13 (1985): 461–72.

"Salvation and Rethinking Mission: Religious Pluralism and the Uniqueness of Christ." *Faith and Mission* 4 (1987): 33–47.

"The Twenty-First Century Church and Worldwide Islam." *Faith and Mission* 11 (1994): 64–80.

"Four Faces of Islam After the Terrorist Attack upon America: A Christian Response." *Faith and Mission* 19 (2002): 3–9.

"World Religions in North Carolina." Co-written with Lisa Grissom in *North Carolina Society's Collection on Religion in North Carolina*. Jefferson, NC: McFarland Publishers, 2018.

Numerous book reviews and articles published in *Journal of Church and State, Theology Today, International Bulletin of Missionary Research, Faith and Mission, Baptist Histo-*

ry and Heritage, Biblical Recorder, Missiology, Nurturing Faith, Baptist Today.
Various articles in Baptist publications including North Carolina, Virginia, Texas, South Carolina, Florida, Georgia and in Southern Baptist Convention publications including Lifeway.

Essays

"Proclaiming Christ to American Religious Groups." In *The Gospel for the New Millennium*, ed. J. Chris Schofield. Nashville: Broadman and Holman 2001.

Audiovisual

Major Religions of the World Nashville, TN: Broadman, 1981.

Dean Bush's Comments at the Retirement Luncheon for Professors Ben Johnson and George Braswell

December 14, 2004

These brief comments can never actually represent what these two men have meant to SEBTS.

Ben and George were both here before I came. They have seen the best and the worst of times. With honesty I can say each played a role in the life of this school that will remain far beyond the ordinary legacy of a faculty member.

Both earned the respect of colleagues then and now. Both men are loved by students then and now.

Both have had uniquely different but equally distinguished careers both here and in former workplaces.

Ben Johnson established the music program at SEBTS. He is not the only teacher over these years, of course! But he laid the foundation for the program we have today. His efforts to reach out to the musical community resulted in marvelous productions of Christmas and Easter music. SEBTS performed the great works and did them well. We combined our small number of student voices with many of those in the community and produced fantastic performances even when our student enrollment was very small. Ben never accepted second place. He always wanted to perform at the highest level possible for the personnel we had.

Ben became a personal friend to me when that was not the most popular thing to do, and he always sought to find a "better" way to handle difficulties. Bonnie was a faithful encourager even when I am sure she did not always feel encouraged. Ben found a way to give himself to Christ through his music. SEBTS again and again received far more than it gave. If Binkley Chapel could talk, it would say that the worshipful atmosphere of today is at least in part an outgrowth of the ministry of Ben Johnson over these many years.

George Braswell is Southeastern's unique contribution to missiology and especially Islamic studies. George knew, long before most of us realized it, that the rise of Islam was the greatest challenge Christianity would face in the 21st Century.

George is uniquely gifted. He is a scholar, an author, an administrator (the DMin program finally found its life when George began to lead it). Few of us have been as prolific as George Braswell. His knowledge of Islam is literally unsurpassed. He has lived the Islamic culture of the Middle East. He has studied it in Southeast Asia and has always evaluated Islam with a balanced Christian witness.

I walked with George through a Buddhist temple school yard in Chiangmai, Thailand, and heard him chat-up the young boys there with stories about Michael Jordan and American basketball, only to leave them with a clear testimony of one greater than Michael Jordan or Buddha.

He sees a temple or a mosque, and before you can blink, he has walked in, met the leader, introduced himself as a professor of world religions in a Christian Seminary, and asked and received permission to bring a group of SEBTS students to visit, listen, and ask questions in the context of a Christian witness in the very environs of the mosque or temple. This happened around the world.

As expert on cults and world religions, he never hides his faith or shies away from a word of Christian witness, for he knows that Christ has the real answers.

"Picky, picky, picky" about the many details and never failing to correct me when he thought I needed it, yet I never felt that George was trying to hurt this school or weaken its impact on the world. He and Joan have surely not been happy with everything they have seen and heard around here, but George always wanted to be on the right side of every issue, even when the cost was high. I have never known anyone else like him. George, you have enriched my life. Thank you.

George Braswell and Ben Johnson. Very different men. Both essential to the history and life of this institution. We will not really let them go. We always need adjunctive teachers, but even more we need their love for truth, for doing what is right, and for service offered not to please men but to please God.

My words do not adequately reflect the deep appreciation I have for both of these men. May God richly bless all that both of you do for Him.

FACULTY PROFILE OF PROFESSOR GEORGE BRASWELL

The following article is from the seminary Outlook magazine of June 2000. The article is titled "Faculty Profile: George Braswell leads Southern Baptists in evangelization of Muslims."

Through colorful carpets draped over chairs and embroidered wall-hangings, professor George W. Braswell, Jr.'s office communicates not only a love for Islamic culture, but an intense desire to bring Muslims to Christ.

As the first Southern Baptist missionary commissioned to Iran in 1967, Braswell pioneered the study of Islam for Southern Baptists, while serving on the faculty of Islamic Theology at the University of Tehran from 1968 to 1974.

Over the past 26 years, Braswell' s heart for Muslims has compelled him to write seven books and a dozen journal articles on the Islamic culture and faith while serving as "Distinguished Professor of Missions and World Religions" at Southeastern Seminary.

His newest book, *What You Need To Know About Islam and Muslims*, published in February by Broadman & Holman, is written for the church lay person. The book provides insight on how to share the Christian faith with Muslims.

"For 35 years I've been interested in the Islamic world," Braswell says as he glances around his office brimming with Islamic artifacts. "Islam is the fastest growing religion in the world, so we've got a lot of people who need to understand (Muslims) and then train themselves to reach out to them."

Braswell's work has garnered him a reputation as one of the premier scholars on Islam.

James T. Draper, Jr., president of LifeWay Christian Resources of the Southern Baptist Convention, describes Braswell as "the greatest evangelical authority on Islam and Muslims in the Southern Baptist Convention."

"He (is) a man really ahead of his time," Draper says. "He was a behind-the-scenes missionary to World A before we knew what World A was."

Recognized internationally as an authority in the area of Islamic studies, Braswell's passion to reach Muslims with the Gospel has carried him throughout the world including Europe, the Middle East, Central America, North and South Africa, Central Asia, Kazakhstan, Uzbekistan and Southeast Asia.

Yet no matter where his travels take him, Braswell's roots run deep on the Wake Forest, N.C. campus where he graduated from Wake Forest College in the 1950s, and later returned to earn a doctor of ministry degree in theology and missions from the seminary in the early 1970s before joining the faculty in 1974.

"This has been a special place," Braswell says. "It was a special place when I was in college, when I was a ministerial student answering God's call to the ministry, and when I was a furloughing missionary retraining myself to go back to the Middle East to be a missionary among Muslims. Listening to God's calling and being faithful to Him has led me here and has led me to stay here."

Last summer, Braswell received the 1999 Distinguished Alumnus Award during the seminary's annual alumni luncheon held in Atlanta, with his wife of 42 years, Joan, by his side.

Paige Patterson, president of Southeastern and the Southern Baptist Convention, describes Braswell as one of the most unique men he's ever known.

Patterson says one can quickly get a sense for what drives Braswell by observing his "unparalleled determination" on the tennis court.

"That exhibited on the tennis court is exactly what you see in the classroom and in everything else." Patterson says. "He is a man who is a genuine scholar and an absolute pleasant joy to have as a part of our faculty team."

In addition to his classroom duties, Braswell serves as director of Southeastern's Doctor of Ministry program, a post he's held since 1991.

As director of the DMin program, Braswell is helping establish a similar program for pastors in the Philippines.

Braswell says the program will give Filipino pastors a chance to retool, regroup and refocus by developing and sharpening their evangelistic skills. This summer, Southeastern will host the new Filipino class for six weeks of training.

As a father of four and grandfather of two, family and education have been mainstays throughout Braswell's life, as he earned a bachelor of divinity from Yale University Divinity School as well as master's and doctoral degrees in cultural anthropology from the University of North Carolina at Chapel Hill.

Braswell says his call to world missions is rooted in his childhood. He became a Christian at the age of 12, having been raised in a mission-minded church.

"My Sunday School teachers were also my elementary school teachers," Braswell says. "They not only taught me as a young boy about Jesus and all the Bible teachings, but I'd go to elementary school and they were my second through fourth grade teachers, leading me along to make sure I was growing up in the church's teachings."

Later, as pastor of Cullowhee Baptist Church in Cullowhee, N.C., from 1962-1967, Braswell instilled a heart for missions to his congregation by inviting missionaries to preach revivals in his church and taking the youth to Foreign Mission Week in Ridgecrest, N.C.

"I would always say to my youth, 'the Lord will call some of you to the mission field,' " Braswell says. "But it ended up that He called my wife and me."

Braswell's heart for international missions, however, begins at home. For more than 20 years, he directed a church planting program at Southeastern which placed students in ministry positions in nearly 30 states throughout the U.S. for 10 weeks each summer.

After years of sharing the Gospel throughout the world, Braswell says the opportunities for global evangelization have never been greater.

About 30 miles from the seminary campus, Braswell leads his "Practicum in World Religions" class on tours of Muslim mosques and Hindu temples in Raleigh, N.C.

"We know Muslims aren't going to come knock on our doors," Braswell says. "But if we can go to where they are, inside the mosques, and actually plant seeds about Jesus, then why not do that? Most of my students will never go to India, but when we go to the Hindu temple in Raleigh, they feel they've been there and begin to understand what our missionaries face. They can imagine our missionaries walking the streets of New Delhi or Bombay to the market place. All the incense smells come to life, and they begin to identify with the missionaries."

King, Melissa. "Faculty Profile: George Braswell leads Southern Baptists in evangelization of Muslims." *The Outlook*, June 2000, 3-4. Internet Archive.

NOTES

President Sydnor L. Stealy
1951–1963

1. "Baptist Official Dr. Stealey Dies," *The News and Observer* (Raleigh), July 26, 1969, Vertical Files, Archives and Special Collections, Library at Southeastern, Southeastern Baptist Theological Seminary, Wake Forest, NC.; Jane Hall, "Dr. Sydnor Stealey: A Seminary Grows at Wake Forest," *The News and Observer* (Raleigh), October 19, 1958, Vertical Files, Archives and Special Collections, Library at Southeastern, Southeastern Baptist Theological Seminary, Wake Forest, NC.

2. "Baptist Official Dr. Stealey Dies," *The News and Observer* (Raleigh), July 26, 1969, Vertical Files, Archives and Special Collections, Library at Southeastern, Southeastern Baptist Theological Seminary, Wake Forest, NC.

3. "In Memoriam: Dr. Sydnor Lorenzo Stealey," (Wake Forest, NC: Southeastern Baptist Theological Seminary, 1970), Vertical Files, Archives and Special Collections, Library at Southeastern, Southeastern Baptist Theological Seminary, Wake Forest, NC.

4. Jane Hall, "Dr. Sydnor Stealey: A Seminary Grows at Wake Forest," *The News and Observer* (Raleigh), October 19, 1958, Vertical Files, Archives and Special Collections, Library at Southeastern, Southeastern Baptist Theological Seminary, Wake Forest, NC.

5. "Biographical Sketch of Dr. Sydnor Lorenzo Stealey, President." Vertical Files, Archives and Special Collections, Library at Southeastern, Southeastern Baptist Theological Seminary, Wake Forest, NC.

6. "Biographical Sketch of Dr. Sydnor Lorenzo Stealey, President," Vertical Files, Archives and Special Collections, Library at Southeastern, Southeastern Baptist Theological Seminary, Wake Forest, NC.

7. "Southeastern Baptist Theological Seminary, Bulletin, July 1951," 11, SEBTS Catalogs - 1950s, Archives and Special Collections, Library at Southeastern, Southeastern Baptist Theological Seminary, Wake Forest, NC.

8. "Southeastern Receives Full Accreditation," *The Outlook,* July 1958, 3, Internet Archive.

9. "Seminary Making Every Effort to Place Students In Pastorates," *Southeastern Seminary Bulletin,* May 1952, 8, Internet Archive.

10. O. T. Binkley, "New Program Set," *Southeastern Seminary Bulletin,* May 1953, 8, Internet Archive.

11. Jane Hall, "Dr. Sydnor Stealey: A Seminary Grows at Wake Forest," *The News and Observer* (Raleigh), October 19, 1958, Vertical Files, Archives and Special Collections, Library at Southeastern, Southeastern Baptist Theological Seminary, Wake Forest, NC.
12. M. Ray McKay, "The Great Relevancy," *The Outlook*, January 1957, 3, Internet Archive.
13. "Seminary Begins Fifth Term," *The Outlook* August 1955, 3, Internet Archive.; "Southeastern Seminary Alumni News, Class of 1955," *The Outlook* August 1955, 5, Internet Archive.
14. "Urgent Need," *The Outlook,* April 1961, 3, Internet Archive.
15. "Southeastern Receives $26,000 Missions Scholarship Fund," *The Outlook,* February 1956, 12, Internet Archives.
16. "Dr. Sydnor Stealey to Retire July 31; Trustees Elect Dean Binkley Successor," *The Outlook,* January-February 1963, 3, Internet Archive.; K. McCormick "Campus Column," *The Outlook,* April 1961, 12, Internet Archive.

President Olin T. Binkley
1963–1974

1. "Biographical Sketch of Olin Trivette Binkley, President-Emeritus," Vertical Files, Archives and Special Collections, Library at Southeastern, Southeastern Baptist Theological Seminary, Wake Forest, NC.

2. "Biographical Sketch of Olin Trivette Binkley, President-Emeritus," Vertical Files, Archives and Special Collections, Library at Southeastern, Southeastern Baptist Theological Seminary, Wake Forest, NC.

3. Jimmy Allen, "Dr. Olin Binkley nurtures Wake Forest and the Seminary," *The Wake Weekly* (Wake Forest), February 2, 1995, Vertical Files, Archives and Special Collections, Library at Southeastern, Southeastern Baptist Theological Seminary, Wake Forest, NC.

4. "Biographical Sketch of Olin Trivette Binkley, President-Emeritus," Vertical Files, Archives and Special Collections, Library at Southeastern, Southeastern Baptist Theological Seminary, Wake Forest, NC.

5. "President's Paragraphs," *The Outlook,* July 1958, 2, Internet Archive.

6. "Dr. Sydnor Stealey to Retire July 31; Trustees Elect Dean Binkley Successor," *The Outlook,* January-February 1963, 3, Internet Archive.; "The Inauguration of Olin Trivette Binkley as Second President: An Historic Day," *The Outlook,* December 1963, 3, Internet Archive.

7. "President of A.A.T.S.," *The Outlook,* September-October 1966, 5, Internet Archive.; "Biographical Sketch of Olin Trivette Binkley, President-Emeritus," Vertical Files, Archives and Special Collections, Library at Southeastern, Southeastern Baptist Theological Seminary, Wake Forest, NC.

8. "Annual Meeting of Board of Trustees," *The Outlook,* March–April 1971, 3, Internet Archive.

9. "President's Paragraphs," *The Outlook,* September–October 1966, 2, Internet Archive.

10. "Special News Flash," *The Outlook,* March–April 1967, 4, Internet Archive.; "New Professor," *The Outlook,* May–June 1966, 8, Internet Archive.

11. "Southeastern Co-Sponsors Urban Study," *The Outlook,* January–February 1967, 3, Internet Archive.; "Urban Studies Seminar," *The Outlook,* September–October 1969, 10, Internet Archive.

12. "Partnership in Learning," *The Outlook,* November–December 1970, 2, Internet Archive.

13. "Urban Studies Seminar," *The Outlook,* September–October 1969, 10, Internet Archive.

14. Phil Royce, "Missionaries At Southeastern," *The Outlook* November–December 1962, 8, Internet Archive.

15. Tom Watkins, "BCH to Receive Books From Binkley Collection," *Charity & Children* 95, no.5 (October 1981): 1, 5, Vertical Files, Archives and Special Collections, Library at Southeastern, Southeastern Baptist Theological Seminary, Wake Forest, NC.

16. Jimmy Allen, "Dr. Olin Binkley nurtures Wake Forest and the Seminary," *The Wake Weekly* (Wake Forest), February 2, 1995, Vertical Files, Archives and Special Collections, Library at Southeastern, Southeastern Baptist Theological Seminary, Wake Forest, NC.

17. "Equipment for Ministry," *The Outlook,* September–October 1969, 2, Internet Archive.

18. "Chapel and Library Building Named," *The Outlook,* March–April 1969, 3, Internet Archive.

President W. Randall Lolley
1974–1988

1. "Vita," Vertical Files, Archives and Special Collections, Library at Southeastern, Southeastern Baptist Theological Seminary, Wake Forest, NC.; "Opening Convocation Fall Semester 1984 Southeastern Baptist Theological Seminary: Celebrating Ten Years of Leadership, President and Mrs. W. Randall Lolley, 1974-1984," (Wake Forest, NC: Southeastern Baptist Theological Seminary, 1984), Vertical Files, Archives and Special Collections, Library at Southeastern, Southeastern Baptist Theological Seminary, Wake Forest, NC.

2. "Vita," Vertical Files, Archives and Special Collections, Library at Southeastern, Southeastern Baptist Theological Seminary, Wake Forest, NC.; "Opening Convocation Fall Semester 1984 Southeastern Baptist Theological Seminary: Celebrating Ten Years of Leadership, President and Mrs. W. Randall Lolley, 1974-1984," (Wake Forest, NC: Southeastern Baptist Theological Seminary, 1984), Vertical Files, Archives and Special Collections, Library at Southeastern, Southeastern Baptist Theological Seminary, Wake Forest, NC.

3. Keith Harper and Steven McKinion, *Then and Now: A Compilation and Celebration of Fifty years at Southeastern Baptist Theological Seminary* (Wake Forest, NC: Southeastern Baptist Theological Seminary),74-75, Archives and Special Collections, Library at Southeastern, Southeastern Baptist Theological Seminary, Wake Forest, NC.

4. "Southeastern Seminary's President-Elect," *The Outlook,* July-August 1974, 3, Internet Archive.

5. "Planning," *The Outlook,* September-October 1977, 2, Internet Archive.; "Forum," *The Outlook,* March-April 1983, 2, Internet Archive.

6. Rodney V. Byard, "Lolley brings down-home style to presidency," *The Wake Weekly* (Wake Forest), May 6, 1982, Vertical Files, Archives and Special Collections, Library at Southeastern, Southeastern Baptist Theological Seminary, Wake Forest, NC.

7. "Campus News," *The Outlook,* March-April 1982, 11, Internet Archive.

8. "Missions Is Our Calling," *The Outlook,* November-December 1984, 4, Internet Archive.

9. "Missions," *The Outlook,* November-December 1979, 2, Internet Archive.; "Practicum in World Religions," *The Outlook,* November-December 1981, 8, Internet Archive.

10. "Missions," *The Outlook,* November-December 1979, 2, Internet Archive.; "Summer Activities," *The Outlook,* September-October 1983, 4, Internet Archive.

11. "Formation in Ministry: A New Look," *The Outlook,* January-February 1979, 3, Internet Archive.

12. "Southeastern to Host January Bible Study Institute November 14," *The Outlook,* September-October 1986, 5, Internet Archive.; "Evening Classes Announced," *The Outlook,* July-August 1982, 7, Internet Archive.

13. "New Professor," *The Outlook,* March-April 1981, 5, Internet Archive.; "Evangelism," *The Outlook,* March-April 1977, 2, Internet Archive.; "Evangelism Ap-

pointment," *The Outlook,* May-June 1978, 8, Internet Archive.

14. "A Statement at the Transition," *The Outlook,* November-December 1987, 2, Internet Archive.; "Outlook, March-April 1988," *The Outlook,* March-April 1988, 4, Internet Archive.

President Lewis A. Drummond
1988–1992

1. "Biographical Data: Lewis A. Drummond, President," Vertical Files, Archives and Special Collections, Library at Southeastern, Southeastern Baptist Theological Seminary, Wake Forest, NC.; "Drummond sees his ministry as a step-by-step process," *The Outlook,* November-December 1988, 4, Internet Archive.

2. "Biographical Data: Lewis A. Drummond, President," Vertical Files, Archives and Special Collections, Library at Southeastern, Southeastern Baptist Theological Seminary, Wake Forest, NC.

3. "Lewis Drummond is Elected President," *The Outlook,* March-April 1988, 3, Internet Archive.; "Biographical Data: Lewis A. Drummond, President," Vertical Files, Archives and Special Collections, Library at Southeastern, Southeastern Baptist Theological Seminary, Wake Forest, NC.

4. "Drummond Becomes 4th President, Promises to 'Take Up Spiritual Mantle,'" *The Outlook,* November-December 1988, 3, Internet Archive.; "Lewis Drummond is

Elected President," *The Outlook*, March–April 1988, 3, Internet Archive.

5. "Breaking New Ground," *The Outlook,* May–June 1989, 2, Internet Archive.

6. "A Heart for the World," *The Outlook,* Spring 1991, 15, Internet Archive.

7. "Southeastern Makes History in Eastern Europe," *The Outlook,* Fall 1990, 13, Internet Archive.; "Romania Calls," *The Outlook,* Fall 1991, 10–11, Internet Archive.

8. "Where Are We Going?" *The Outlook,* January–February 1989, 2, Internet Archive.

9. "Where Are We Going?" *The Outlook,* January–February 1989, 2, Internet Archive.; "Trustees Respond to Drummond's Retirement," *The Outlook,* Spring 1992, 3, Internet Archive.

10. "President's Message," *The Outlook,* Fall 1992, 2, Internet Archive.

11. "Message For The Holidays," *The Outlook,* Winter 1989, 2, Internet Archive.; "Up-Date: Lewis Drummond," *The Outlook,* Winter 1990, 10, Internet Archive.

12. "In Parting," *The Outlook,* Spring 1992, 2, Internet Archive.

13. Keith Harper and Steven McKinion, *Then and Now: A Compilation and Celebration of Fifty years at Southeastern Baptist Theological Seminary* (Wake Forest, NC: Southeastern Baptist Theological Seminary, 2000), 109, Archives and Special Collections, Library at Southeastern, Southeastern Baptist Theological Seminary, Wake Forest, NC.

President L. Paige Patterson
1992-2003

1. Keith Harper and Steven McKinion, *Then and Now: A Compilation and Celebration of Fifty years at Southeastern Baptist Theological Seminary* (Wake Forest, NC: Southeastern Baptist Theological Seminary, 2000), 113, Archives and Special Collections, Library at Southeastern, Southeastern Baptist Theological Seminary, Wake Forest, NC.

2. Lisa Bellamy, "Patterson's gospel: Inerrancy with an open ear," *The News and Observer* (Raleigh), May 13, 1992, reprint, Vertical Files, Archives and Special Collections, Library at Southeastern, Southeastern Baptist Theological Seminary, Wake Forest, NC.

3. "Paige Patterson: President, Southeastern Baptist Theological Seminary," Vertical Files, Archives and Special Collections, Library at Southeastern, Southeastern Baptist Theological Seminary, Wake Forest, NC.; Keith Harper and Steven McKinion, *Then and Now: A Compilation and Celebration of Fifty years at Southeastern Baptist Theological Seminary* (Wake Forest, NC: Southeastern Baptist Theological Seminary, 2000), 113, Archives and Special Collections, Library at Southeastern, Southeastern Baptist Theological Seminary, Wake Forest, NC.

4. "President's Message," *The Outlook,* Fall 1992, 2, Internet Archive.; Harper, Keith and Steven McKinion. *Then and Now: A Compilation and Celebration of Fifty years at Southeastern Baptist Theological Seminary* (Wake

Forest, NC: Southeastern Baptist Theological Seminary, 2000), 112, Archives and Special Collections, Library at Southeastern, Southeastern Baptist Theological Seminary, Wake Forest, NC.

5. Norman Miller, "Trustees Celebrate Endowment; Approve Curriculum Changes," *The Outlook,* Spring–Summer 1994, 11, Internet Archive.; Dwayne Hastings, "Forward, into the past: SEBTS returns to Classical Theological Training," *The Outlook,* Fall 1994, 3, Internet Archive.; "Trustees Form New College," *The Outlook,* Winter 1994, 1, Internet Archive.; "Green Light for Ph.D. Program," *The Outlook,* Winter 1994, 4, Internet Archive.; "Trustees Approve Counseling Degree," *The Outlook,* Summer 1995, 3, Internet Archive.

6. "SEBTS and FMB Cosponsor Church Planting Degree," *The Outlook,* Winter 1994, 5, Internet Archive.; "The Journey," *The Outlook,* June 2000, Internet Archive.

7. "Southeastern Partnership Canvasses New Hampshire with New Churches," *The Outlook,* June 2001, 7, Internet Archive.; "President's Message," *The Outlook,* Summer 1993, 2, Internet Archive.

8. "Calling Out the Called," *The Outlook,* Spring 2002, 3, Internet Archive.

9. "Southeastern Accreditation Reaffirmed By Southern Association of Colleges and Schools," *The Outlook,* Winter 1993, 3, Internet Archive,; Jon Walker, "Enrollment Dramatically Increases," *The Outlook,* Winter 1993, 4, Internet Archive.

10. Norman Miller, "Trustees Celebrate Endowment; Approve Curriculum Changes," *The Outlook,* Spring-Summer 1994, 11, Internet Archive.

11. "Directors of Great Commission Center Announced," *The Outlook*, Summer 1993, 5, Internet Archive.; "Campus Improvements," *The Outlook,* June 2001, 9, Internet Archive.

12. "N.C. Newspaper Lists Patterson Among Visionaries," *The Outlook,* June 2000, 5, Internet Archive.

13. Evan Lenow, "Patterson says 'goodbye,'" *Newsline*, August 25, 2003. Vol 4 Is 1., 1, Vertical Files, Archives and Special Collections, Library at Southeastern, Southeastern Baptist Theological Seminary, Wake Forest, NC.

Interim President Bart C. Neal
2003–2004

1. Jerry Higgins, "Neal named interim president," *Newsline*, August 25, 2003, 1, 3, Vertical Files, Archives and Special Collections, Library at Southeastern, Southeastern Baptist Theological Seminary, Wake Forest, NC.; "Biographical Information," Vertical Files, Archives and Special Collections, Library at Southeastern, Southeastern Baptist Theological Seminary, Wake Forest, NC.

2. "Biographical Information," Vertical Files, Archives and Special Collections, Library at Southeastern, Southeastern Baptist Theological Seminary, Wake Forest, NC.

3. Jerry Higgins, "Neal named interim president," *Newsline*,

August 25, 2003, 1, 3, Vertical Files, Archives and Special Collections, Library at Southeastern, Southeastern Baptist Theological Seminary, Wake Forest, NC.; "New Faces at Southeastern," *The Outlook,* Fall 1993, 9, Internet Archive.

4. Jason Hall, "Allen Elected Advancement VP," *The Outlook,* Spring 2005, 20, Internet Archive.

President Daniel L. Akin
2004–Present

1. "The Head, The Heart, The Hands: The Vision of Daniel L. Akin," *The Outlook,* Spring 2004, 18, Internet Archive.; "A Letter from the President," *The Great Commission Magazine of Southeastern Baptist Theological Seminary,* Spring 2016, 3, Issuu.

2. "A Letter from the President," *The Great Commission Magazine of Southeastern Baptist Theological Seminary,* Spring 2016, 3, Issuu.

3. "The Head, The Heart, The Hands: The Vision of Daniel L. Akin," *The Outlook,* Spring 2004, 18, Internet Archive.; "About," Danny Akin: President, Southeastern Seminary, last modified April 2021, https://www.danielakin.com/about/.

4. "About," Danny Akin: President, Southeastern Seminary, last modified April 2021, https://www.danielakin.com/about/.

5. "Faculty Profile: Dr. Danny Akin," *The Outlook,* Winter 1993, 10–11, Internet Archive.

6. "About," Danny Akin: President, Southeastern Seminary, last modified April 2021, https://www.danielakin.com/about/.

7. "Trustees affirm statements, approve degree changes," *The Outlook,* Spring 2004, 14, Internet Archive.; "About," Danny Akin: President, Southeastern Seminary, last modified April 2021, https://www.danielakin.com/about/.

8. "The President's Heart: All for the Glory of God," *The Outlook,* Spring 2004, 4, Internet Archive.

9. "A Great Commission Seminary," *The Outlook,* Fall 2006, 3, Internet Archive.

10. "Why We Teach and Preach the Infallible and Inerrant Word of God in an Expository Manner," *The Great Commission Magazine of Southeastern Baptist Theological Seminary,* Spring 2017, 3, Issuu.

11. "Preparing to Go," *The Outlook,* Fall 2007, 2, Internet Archive.; "Board of Visitors and Trustees Gather to Hear about Those Being Sent," *The Great Commission Magazine of Southeastern Baptist Theological Seminary,* Spring 2013, 8, Issuu.

12. "North Carolina Field Minister Program Holds First Convocation Service," *The Great Commission Magazine of Southeastern Baptist Theological Seminary,* Fall 2017, 17, Issuu.

13. Lauren Crane, "The Global Theological Initiative," *The Outlook,* Spring 2011, 9-11, Issuu.; "East Asian Leadership Initiative Begins at Southeastern," *The Great Commission Magazine of Southeastern Baptist Theological*

Seminary, Fall 2018, 10, Issuu.; "Southeastern Welcomes New Director of Hispanic Leadership Development," *The Great Commission Magazine of Southeastern Baptist Theological Seminary,* Spring 2017, 14, Issuu.; "Southeastern Begins New Persian Leadership Program," *The Great Commission Magazine of Southeastern Baptist Theological Seminary,* Spring 2017, 14, Issuu.

14. For a full list of book publications see https://www.danielakin.com/books/books/.

Bibliography

"About." Danny Akin: President, Southeastern Seminary, last modified April 2021. https://www.danielakin. com/about/.

"A Great Commission Seminary." *The Outlook,* Fall 2006. Internet Archive.

"A Heart for the World." *The Outlook,* Spring 1991. Internet Archive.

"A Letter from the President." *The Great Commission Magazine of Southeastern Baptist Theological Seminary,* Spring 2016. Issuu.

Allen, Jimmy. "Dr. Olin Binkley nurtures Wake Forest and the Seminary." *The Wake Weekly* Wake Forest, February 2, 1995. Vertical Files, Archives and Special Collections, Library at Southeastern, Southeastern Baptist Theological Seminary, Wake Forest, NC.

"Annual Meeting of Board of Trustees." *The Outlook,* March–April 1971. Internet Archive.

"A Statement at the Transition." *The Outlook,* November–December 1987. Internet Archive.

"Baptist Official Dr. Stealey Dies." *The News and Observer*, Raleigh, July 26, 1969. Vertical Files, Archives and Special Collections, Library at Southeastern, Southeastern Baptist Theological Seminary, Wake Forest, NC.

Bellamy, Lisa. "Patterson's gospel: Inerrancy with an open ear." *The News and Observer*, Raleigh, May 13, 1992, reprint. Vertical Files, Archives and Special Collections, Library at Southeastern, Southeastern Baptist Theological Seminary, Wake Forest, NC.

Binkley, O. T. "New Program Set." *Southeastern Seminary Bulletin,* May 1953. Internet Archive.

"Biographical Data: Lewis A. Drummond, President," Lewis A. Drummond - Vertical Files, Archives and Special Collections, Library at Southeastern, Southeastern Baptist Theological Seminary, Wake Forest, NC.

"Biographical Information." Bart Neal - Vertical Files, Archives and Special Collections, Library at Southeastern, Southeastern Baptist Theological Seminary, Wake Forest, NC.

"Biographical Sketch of Dr. Sydnor Lorenzo Stealey, President." Sydnor L. Stealey - Vertical Files, Archives and Special Collections, Library at Southeastern,

Southeastern Baptist Theological Seminary, Wake Forest, NC.

"Biographical Sketch of Olin Trivette Binkley, President-Emeritus." Olin T. Binkley - Vertical Files, Archives and Special Collections, Library at Southeastern, Southeastern Baptist Theological Seminary, Wake Forest, NC.

"Board of Visitors and Trustees Gather to Hear about Those Being Sent." *The Great Commission Magazine of Southeastern Baptist Theological Seminary,* Spring 2013. Issuu.

"Breaking New Ground." *The Outlook,* May-June 1989. Internet Archive.

Byard, Rodney V. "Lolley brings down-home style to presidency." *The Wake Weekly*, Wake Forest, May 6, 1982. Vertical Files, Archives and Special Collections, Library at Southeastern, Southeastern Baptist Theological Seminary, Wake Forest, NC.

"Calling Out the Called." *The Outlook,* Spring 2002. Internet Archive.

"Campus Improvements." *The Outlook,* June 2001. Internet Archive.

"Campus News." *The Outlook,* March-April 1982. Internet Archive.

"Chapel and Library Building Named." *The Outlook,* March-April 1969. Internet Archive. Crane, Lauren. "The Global Theological Initiative." *The Outlook,* Spring 2011. Issuu.

"Directors of Great Commission Center Announced." *The Outlook*, Summer 1993. Internet Archive.

"Dr. Sydnor Stealey to Retire July 31; Trustees Elect Dean Binkley Successor." *The Outlook,* January– February 1963. Internet Archive.

"Drummond Becomes 4th President, Promises to 'Take Up Spiritual Mantle.'" *The Outlook,* November– December 1988. Internet Archive.

"Drummond sees his ministry as a step-by-step process." *The Outlook,* November-December 1988. Internet Archive.

"East Asian Leadership Initiative Begins at Southeastern." *The Great Commission Magazine of Southeastern Baptist Theological Seminary,* Fall 2018. Issuu.

"Equipment for Ministry." *The Outlook,* September-October 1969. Internet Archive.

"Evangelism." *The Outlook,* March–April 1977. Internet Archive.

"Evangelism Appointment." *The Outlook,* May-June 1978. Internet Archive.

"Evening Classes Announced." *The Outlook,* July-August 1982. Internet Archive.

"Faculty Profile: Dr. Danny Akin." *The Outlook,* Winter 1993. Internet Archive.

"Formation in Ministry: A New Look." *The Outlook,* January-February 1979. Internet Archive.

"Forum." *The Outlook,* March-April 1983. Internet Archive.

"Green Light for Ph.D. Program." *The Outlook,* Winter 1994. Internet Archive.

Hall, Jane. "Dr. Sydnor Stealey: A Seminary Grows at Wake Forest." *The News and Observer*, Raleigh, October 19, 1958. Vertical Files, Archives and Special Collections, Library at Southeastern, Southeastern Baptist Theological Seminary, Wake Forest, NC.

Hall, Jason. "Allen Elected Advancement VP." *The Outlook,* Spring 2005. Internet Archive.

Harper, Keith and Steven McKinion. *Then and Now: A Compilation and Celebration of Fifty years at Southeastern Baptist Theological Seminary*. Wake Forest, NC: Southeastern Baptist Theological Seminary, 2000. Archives and Special Collections, Library at Southeastern, Southeastern Baptist Theological Seminary, Wake Forest, NC.

Hastings, Dwayne. "Forward, into the past: SEBTS returns to Classical Theological Training." *The Outlook,* Fall 1994. Internet Archive.

Higgins, Jerry. "Neal named interim president." *Newsline*, August 25, 2003. Vertical Files, Archives and Special Collections, Library at Southeastern, Southeastern Baptist Theological Seminary, Wake Forest, NC.

"In Memoriam: Dr. Sydnor Lorenzo Stealey." Wake Forest, NC: Southeastern Baptist Theological Seminary, 1970. Vertical Files, Archives and Special Collections, Library at Southeastern, Southeastern Baptist Theological Seminary, Wake Forest, NC.

"In Parting." *The Outlook,* Spring 1992. Internet Archive.

Lenow, Evan. "Patterson says 'goodbye.'" *Newsline*, August 25, 2003. Vol 4 Is 1. Vertical Files, Archives and Special Collections, Library at Southeastern, Southeastern Baptist Theological Seminary, Wake Forest, NC.

"Lewis Drummond is Elected President." *The Outlook,* March–April 1988. Internet Archive.

McCormick, K. "Campus Column." *The Outlook,* April 1961. Internet Archive.

McKay, M. Ray. "The Great Relevancy." *The Outlook,* January 1957. Internet Archive.

"Message For The Holidays." *The Outlook,* Winter 1989. Internet Archive.

Miller, Norman. "Trustees Celebrate Endowment; Approve Curriculum Changes." *The Outlook,* Spring- Summer 1994. Internet Archive.

"Missions." *The Outlook,* November–December 1979. Internet Archive.

"Missions Is Our Calling." *The Outlook,* November–December 1984. Internet Archive.

"N.C. Newspaper Lists Patterson Among Visionaries." *The Outlook,* June 2000. Internet Archive.

"New Faces at Southeastern." *The Outlook,* Fall 1993. Internet Archive.

"New Professor." *The Outlook,* May-June 1966. Internet Archive.

"New Professor." *The Outlook,* March-April 1981. Internet Archive.

"North Carolina Field Minister Program Holds First Convocation Service." *The Great Commission Magazine of Southeastern Baptist Theological Seminary,* Fall 2017. Issuu.

"Opening Convocation Fall Semester 1984 Southeastern Baptist Theological Seminary: Celebrating Ten Years of Leadership, President and Mrs. W. Randall Lolley, 1974-1984." Wake Forest, NC: Southeastern Baptist Theological Seminary, 1984. Vertical Files, Archives and Special Collections, Library at Southeastern, Southeastern Baptist Theological Seminary, Wake Forest, NC.

"Outlook, March-April 1988." *The Outlook,* March-April 1988. Internet Archive.

"Paige Patterson: President, Southeastern Baptist Theological Seminary." Paige Patterson - Vertical Files, Archives and Special Collections, Library at Southeastern, Southeastern Baptist Theological Seminary, Wake Forest, NC.

"Partnership in Learning." *The Outlook,* November-December 1970. Internet Archive.

"Planning." *The Outlook,* September-October 1977. Internet Archive.

"Practicum in World Religions." *The Outlook,* November-December 1981. Internet Archive.

"President of A.A.T.S." *The Outlook,* September-October 1966. Internet Archive.

"Preparing to Go." *The Outlook,* Fall 2007. Internet Archive.

"President's Message." *The Outlook,* Fall 1992. Internet Archive.

"President's Message." *The Outlook,* Summer 1993. Internet Archive.

"President's Paragraphs." *The Outlook,* July 1958. Internet Archive.

"President's Paragraphs." *The Outlook,* September-October 1966. Internet Archive.

"Romania Calls." *The Outlook,* Fall 1991. Internet Archive.

Royce, Phil. "Missionaries At Southeastern." *The Outlook* November-December 1962. Internet Archive.

"SEBTS and FMB Cosponsor Church Planting Degree." *The Outlook,* Winter 1994. Internet Archive.

"Seminary Begins Fifth Term." *The Outlook* August 1955. Internet Archive.

"Seminary Making Every Effort to Place Students In Pastorates." *Southeastern Seminary Bulletin,* May 1952. Internet Archive.

"Southeastern Accreditation Reaffirmed By Southern Association of Colleges and Schools." *The Outlook,* Winter 1993. Internet Archive.

"Southeastern Baptist Theological Seminary, Bulletin, July 1951." SEBTS Catalogs - 1950s, Archives and Special Collections, Library at Southeastern, Southeastern Baptist Theological Seminary, Wake Forest, NC.

"Southeastern Begins New Persian Leadership Program." *The Great Commission Magazine of Southeastern Baptist Theological Seminary,* Spring 2017. Issuu.

"Southeastern Co-Sponsors Urban Study." *The Outlook,* January-February 1967. Internet Archive.

"Southeastern Makes History in Eastern Europe." *The Outlook,* Fall 1990. Internet Archive.

"Southeastern Partnership Canvasses New Hampshire with New Churches." *The Outlook,* June 2001. Internet Archive.

"Southeastern Receives Full Accreditation." *The Outlook,* July 1958. Internet Archive.

"Southeastern Receives $26,000 Missions Scholarship Fund." *The Outlook,* February 1956. Internet Archives.

"Southeastern Seminary Alumni News, Class of 1955." *The Outlook* August 1955. Internet Archive.

"Southeastern Seminary's President-Elect." *The Outlook,* July-August 1974. Internet Archive.

"Southeastern to Host January Bible Study Institute November 14." *The Outlook,* September-October 1986. Internet Archive.

"Southeastern Welcomes New Director of Hispanic Leadership Development." *The Great Commission Mag-*

azine of Southeastern Baptist Theological Seminary, Spring 2017. Issuu.

"Special News Flash." *The Outlook,* March–April 1967. Internet Archive.

"Summer Activities." *The Outlook,* September–October 1983. Internet Archive.

"The Head, The Heart, The Hands: The Vision of Daniel L. Akin." *The Outlook,* Spring 2004. Internet Archive.

"The Inauguration of Olin Trivette Binkley as Second President: An Historic Day." *The Outlook,* December 1963. Internet Archive.

"The Journey." *The Outlook,* June 2000. Internet Archive.

"The President's Heart: All for the Glory of God." *The Outlook,* Spring 2004. Internet Archive.

"Trustees affirm statements, approve degree changes." *The Outlook,* Spring 2004. Internet Archive.

"Trustees Approve Counseling Degree." *The Outlook,* Summer 1995. Internet Archive.

"Trustees Form New College." *The Outlook,* Winter 1994. Internet Archive.

"Trustees Respond to Drummond's Retirement." *The Outlook,* Spring 1992. Internet Archive.

"Up-Date: Lewis Drummond." *The Outlook,* Winter 1990. Internet Archive.

"Urban Studies Seminar." *The Outlook,* September–October 1969. Internet Archive.

"Urgent Need." *The Outlook,* April 1961. Internet Archive.

"Vita." W. Randall Lolley - Vertical Files, Archives and Special Collections, Library at Southeastern, Southeastern Baptist Theological Seminary, Wake Forest, NC.

Walker, Jon. "Enrollment Dramatically Increases." *The Outlook,* Winter 1993. Internet Archive.

Watkins, Tom. "BCH to Receive Books From Binkley Collection." *Charity & Children* 95, no.5 October 1981. Vertical Files, Archives and Special Collections, Library at Southeastern, Southeastern Baptist Theological Seminary, Wake Forest, NC.

"Where Are We Going?" *The Outlook,* January-February 1989. Internet Archive.

"Why We Teach and Preach the Infallible and Inerrant Word of God in an Expository Manner." *The Great Commission Magazine of Southeastern Baptist Theological Seminary,* Spring 2017. Issuu.

Sources for Chapel Talks and Lectures by the Presidents

To access chapel and special event recordings of the seminary presidents, search for selected presidents' names at archives.sebts.edu.